I0048810

ADVANCE PRAISE

"Finally, a self-help book that helps! Most work-life balance books fail to address adequately the issue of money management. Not ENRICH. This book prioritizes financial security and offers a realistic and easy-to-implement strategy for building passive income. Todd Miller speaks from experience."

—MICHELLE TANMIZI, AUTHOR OF BESTSELLER NOVEL, *LATE DAWN*; RETIRED FROM BUSINESS LIFE AT 40

"We have been taught a lot about how to manage our businesses, but not nearly enough on how to manage our lives. Todd Miller is full of creative, provocative, valuable ideas. ENRICH offers useful tools to greater fulfilment. At this moment when the world faces multiple disruptions, we all need this book more than ever."

—RICKY OW, PRESIDENT, WARNERMEDIA ENTERTAINMENT NETWORKS ASIA PACIFIC

"Companies need effective and sustainable strategies to win. Professionals also need strategies to flourish. Todd Miller has spent two decades probing, researching, and experimenting with effective strategies to enrich life."

—M. ERIC JOHNSON, DEAN AND PROFESSOR OF STRATEGY, VANDERBILT UNIVERSITY OWEN GRADUATE SCHOOL OF MANAGEMENT

"Todd Miller faced a dilemma familiar to many professionals: promotion or parenthood. ENRICH lays out an actionable, relevant framework to enrich your life personally, professionally, and financially."

—LAURENCE BATES, GENERAL COUNSEL AND
FIRST NON-JAPANESE DIRECTOR, PANASONIC
CORPORATION; PROUD FATHER OF TWO

"A practical solution for the 24/7 grind. Todd Miller has experimented with reimagining the work-life equation. In these roller-coaster times, we can benefit from some enrichment."

—LOUISA WONG, EXECUTIVE CHAIRMAN, GLOBAL
SAGE, A LEADING INTERNATIONAL EXECUTIVE
SEARCH FIRM HEADQUARTERED IN HONG KONG

"With steely determination and resolve, Todd Miller has achieved what many of us can only dream about: he has arrived at a place where he really is in control of his life. And his happiness is palpable. This book recounts that journey. I urge you to read it."

—SIMON POLLOCK, MANAGING DIRECTOR, INTERNATIONAL,
SUCHERMAN GROUP, LONDON; A MEDIA AND ENTERTAINMENT
INDUSTRY VETERAN, POLLOCK HAS HELD SENIOR
INTERNATIONAL ROLES AT DISNEY, SONY, AND A&E NETWORKS

"Most self-help books about work-life balance talk a big game but come up short on particulars. Not this one. ENRICH doesn't pretend money isn't important or that it will somehow magically appear if you simply pursue your passion. This book gets down to business and shows you what school never did—how to tackle financial freedom."

—GENE SOO, HEAD OF ECOSYSTEM, MAJOR PUBLICLY
LISTED COMPANY AND A STARTUP ECOSYSTEM BUILDER

"Everyone should have a mentor like Todd guiding them through life. While continuing to build a strong family, financial security, and never letting down his colleagues, Todd managed to take two sabbaticals. This is a testament to Todd's ability to innovate the work-life equation."

—SUPERNA KALLE, EXECUTIVE VICE PRESIDENT,
INTERNATIONAL DIGITAL NETWORKS, STARZ, A
LIONSGATE COMPANY, LOS ANGELES

"After reading this book, I was able to bounce back from a job loss by using the ENRICH strategies to take control of my career, my finances, and my personal life. If I had learned these lessons in business school, I can only imagine where I would be at this point financially and professionally. It's never too late to enrich."

—ALEX STRAH, SENIOR TECH EXECUTIVE,
SILICON VALLEY STARTUP

"ENRICH reignited the youthful passion and drive that had slowly faded over the course of my career. It showed me that I was caught in a trap of my own making, and it gave me a step-by-step guide on how to actualize the life I have long desired."

—JOHNNY D., IVY LEAGUE GRADUATE, AGE 32

"I love this book because it combines solid practical business insight sprinkled with spirituality and mixed with interesting personal anecdotes. It's the perfect recipe to inspire and ignite possibilities for one's future."

—JENNIFER TAKAKI, DOCUMENTARY FILMMAKER, NEW YORK

"ENRICH has so much to offer that I read it twice. The book inspired me to embark upon the career I always wanted, but never felt confident or compelled to pursue—until now. Thank you!"

—MICHAEL MARCH, INTERNATIONAL LAWYER, C-SUITE
MEDIA EXECUTIVE, ENTREPRENEUR, AND NOW ACTOR

"*The ENRICH formula future-proofs financial security and champions life success. It's a powerful message—the right words at the right time from the right guy.*"

—SABINA ASTNER, AWARD-WINNING DESIGNER, MUNICH

"*This is a measured and intelligent answer to anybody thinking: "There must be more to life than this, surely?"*"

—TASHAN MEHTA, NOVELIST AND AUTHOR, *THE LIAR'S WEAVE*

"*When it comes to the game of life, ENRICH showed me how to flip the game board over.*"

—DAVID SMITH, AUDITOR, NEW YORK

ENRICH

CREATE WEALTH IN
TIME, MONEY, AND MEANING

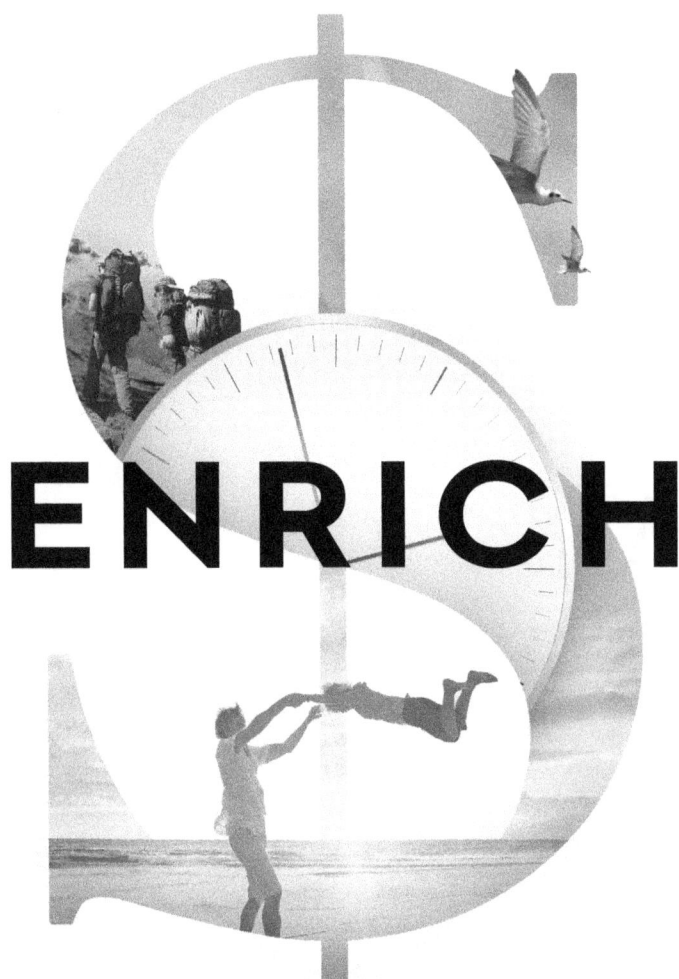

ENRICH

TODD MILLER

LIONCREST
PUBLISHING

To my father, who teaches there is no dress rehearsal.

To my mother-in-law, whose sudden passing reminds, It's About Time.

CONTENTS

ACKNOWLEDGMENTS

It takes a village to produce a book. At least this particular book. I owe much to many who helped shape *ENRICH* and give this project life and resonance.

Special thanks to my immediate family—Patrick and Huey—who politely accommodated this persistent intruder into our lives, like a guest who overstays his welcome.

This book's development spanned years. Susan Patnaik helped pull these strategies into form and function at the front end and in the final stretch. Michael March helped fine-tune the messaging over three separate iterations of this manuscript. Michael gave it to me straight and questioned everything with his lawyerly instincts and substantial wisdom. Alex Strah thoroughly tested and validated these strategies and inspired much of the final chapter. Susan, Michael, and Alex went out of their way to contribute to this book. They immensely enriched *ENRICH*.

A special thank you to the beta readers who *endured* a sprawling, messy early draft. Their time generosity and patience in wading through this first iteration yielded considerable constructive feedback and produced a better book. Thank you Johnny Dryman, J. B. Hsu, Ken Jacquin, Albert Kuo, Michael March, Stephen Ong, Alex Strah, Jennifer Takaki, and Joanna Tan.

Friends across four continents graciously served as a virtual focus group that provided real-time and brutally honest feedback. Thank you Steve Chu, Jenny Chua, Jim Crump, Allen Feng, Tim Hoffman, Albert Kuo, Michael March, John Miller, Katie Enterline Miller, Stephen Ong, David Pan, Susan Patnaik, Gene Soo, Jennifer Takaki, Brad Wilson, Jacob Wong, and Laura Wong. A shout-out also to dozens of members of the Columbia and Vanderbilt communities who volunteered timely input.

Many professionals contributed perspective and life experience as I did my background research. Hearing other people's insightful, inspiring stories helped me give voice to my own. Thank you to H.K. Ang, Annabelle Bond, Danny Burke, Jeremy Butler, Ronna Chao, Jenny Chua, Diana David, David Gething, Adrian Hayes, Paul Heffner, Alan Hodges, Ann Bridgewater Hsu, Carla Jeffrey, Ophelia Ngan, Sylvia Noronha, Charles Scott, Bert Shi, SuSan Tan, Michelle Tanmizi, Fanny Wong, Laura Wong, and Airin Zainul.

The excellent team at Scribe provided just the right amount of handholding to get this book over the finish line. Thank you Emily Anderson, Rachel Brandenburg, Hal Clifford, Rikki Jump, Tucker Max, Carolyn Purnell, Jenny Shipley, and Kayla Sokol. In particular, Tashan Mehta's beautiful editing packs a powerful punch. She was looking out for you, dear reader, to ensure a seamless reading experience. Tashan taught me about narrative, flow, and unpacking complex ideas.

Sasha Sakhnevich and Matt Young produced the elegant graphics.

Finally, reader, thank YOU. I respect your time and have done my best to make this book a worthy investment.

INTRODUCTION

I sketched my first Life Plan on a piece of scratch paper in the middle of the night, while sitting on the Dubai airport floor awaiting a connecting flight.

In January 2020, twenty-four years to the day after I created that first Life Plan, I traded the fast life of Hong Kong for the beach life of Thailand, the country I now call home. I did not just change the scenery or change the pace of life. I shifted to a lifestyle that I anticipated and planned twenty-four years earlier.

On the same day I relocated to Thailand, I received a frantic text message from a good friend seeking some fast career and financial advice. He just lost his job in a company reshuffling. With a family to support, kids in private school, and a mortgage to service, he would imminently lose his only source of income.

He needed some help.

I fully empathized with my friend's situation. I had been there too.

Connecting the dots between writing that first Life Plan and kicking back to a tropical lifestyle forms the philosophy of this book. I discovered early in my career that while "higher" education prepares us for prestigious careers, we are often unprepared to lead meaningful lives. What constitutes a purposeful life, anyway? Business schools teach corporate finance but skip personal finance. If we make enough money, the notion goes, we will eventually figure it out. Eventually.

In other words, we have to wing it.

Since those hours on the Dubai airport floor, I have spent much of my adult life experimenting with the work-life equation. I have pursued answers to some salient questions:

Career is important, but is it enough? Is career an end or a means?

What do I want to accomplish? What is my legacy?

What constitutes an optimal life? How can I enhance my quality of life?

What is success and how much is enough?

How do I prevent work from crowding out life?

How do I insulate myself from a significant shock, such as job loss or market crash?

Some books might teach you how to get rich quick or even how to retire early. Some books might instruct you on how to advance your career or improve productivity in the workplace. This book is more ambitious. This book guides you to take control, "own" your future, and enrich your life.

ENRICH is a methodology that empowers you to design an aspirational plan and live it. This process takes a corporate approach to personal optimization using time-honored business techniques. For many professionals, money is frequently the elephant in the room when it comes to work-life discussions. ENRICH embraces this elephant. ENRICH future-proofs financial security to mitigate dependence upon a paycheck. This creates optionality at work and in life.

The outcome? You liberate your time. You build **time wealth** in addition to **financial wealth**. Most importantly, this method helps you to create **meaning** by igniting your biggest, boldest life goals.

In researching this book, I investigated best practices and current research across many disciplines. I interviewed professionals around the world from a spectrum of backgrounds. These individuals achieve professional success *and* live exuberantly.

I then went further. I spoke with several holders of *multiple* world records to dig into how they set and actualize compelling goals. There's much to learn from the first, fastest, or the sole person on the planet to accomplish something.

You will also learn from the pain I endured and the insights I gained during a corporate career. For a quarter century, I have run multimillion-dollar businesses. This includes eight years as CEO of Asia's largest independent regional broadcaster and a lengthy track record in senior leadership with a major Hollywood studio, where I had responsibility for one of the world's fastest-growing regions.

Through the organizations I have run, I have helped to entertain tens of millions of consumers. I have negotiated international joint ventures, lobbied foreign governments, collaborated with billionaires and celebrities, and launched new businesses. I have also maneuvered through massive technological disruption and industry consolidation.

And I have confronted more corporate BS than anyone deserves in a lifetime.

For a kid from Kentucky, I've been blessed with a colorful career. But it is probably my experiences outside the office that best equipped me to write this book. During my corporate tenure, I managed to:

- ⑤ Jump off the career ladder twice to enjoy sabbaticals
- ⑤ Create a family through adoption
- ⑤ Organize epic annual extended family vacations all over the world
- ⑤ Cycle coast-to-coast across two continents
- ⑤ Raise substantial money for Asian children's charities
- ⑤ Explore more than one hundred countries on all seven continents
- ⑤ Construct a dream beach house
- ⑤ Experiment aggressively with traditional work structures

These experiences helped me formulate and refine the ENRICH concepts, all of which are in this book. Following these principles, I fully retired at the early-ish age of fifty-three—I'm enormously grateful for this privilege. Although my initial plan took twenty-four years to completely realize, the ENRICH strategies can also work on a more compressed timeline. SuSan Tan, who you'll meet in chapter 5, used the ENRICH principles to turn around her life in three years. In chapter 13 you'll read about Alex Strah, the friend who sent that panicky text the day I relocated to Thailand. Facing the worst employment market since the Depression, he used the ENRICH principles to turn around a job loss in just four months. As you go through this book and read the stories of individuals who've benefited from this perspective, you'll see that the stress-tested ENRICH process works. In success, this method transforms.

Fast forward to March 2020, two months after I relocated to Thailand. COVID-19 had infected everything and gut-punched the economy: lives and livelihoods disrupted at light speed, millions of jobs and trillions of dollars wiped out.

It is hard to find anything good about the pandemic pandemonium of 2020, and the pain and hardship this virus has unleashed. And yet, amidst all the wreckage, we find a clarifying opportunity. An opportunity to rethink, rebuild, and rejuvenate our lives and our careers—and to envision a new, enriched normal.

If there is a positive outcome from the viral and economic pandemics of 2020, I posit it will be this: 20/20 clarity about what matters most. The world has changed dramatically, but the principals of life success haven't.

I wrote this book to provide a framework that helps people enrich their lives financially, professionally, and personally. This book is for professionals like my good friend Alex Strah, a well-educated, well-off, successful high achiever dealing with a significant life disruption. Just as it helped Strah, this framework can help you nurture life success and financial security—whether you're starting your first job, approaching the pinnacle of your career, thinking about what follows, or facing a big decision. It is never too late or too early to enrich your life.

While many things changed in 2020, the relevance, validity,

and immediacy of these principles hold steadfast. In this post-pandemic world, perhaps now more than ever, we can all benefit from some enrichment. The goal is not to have it all, but to Ignite all that matters.

CHAPTER 1

MONDAY MORNING MALAISE

"America's Professional Elite: Wealthy, Successful, and Miserable."

—*The New York Times* headline, February 21, 2019

"Sunday Night is the New Monday Morning, and Workers are Miserable."

—*The Wall Street Journal* headline, July 7, 2019

February 2011—I flew to company headquarters in Los Angeles with the expectation and giddy hope that I would be fired. There were rumors that another round of corporate restructuring was around the corner, and I detected subtle signals. I wanted it to happen. I needed it to happen. I was *confident* it would happen.

My boss scheduled a 5 p.m. meeting on a Friday afternoon, my last session that week in LA. An encouraging sign, I thought. A classic HR move. All week I gleefully anticipated that meeting the way a child looks forward to Christmas morning. I eagerly awaited a golden parachute. I fantasized about how I would play the victim. How I would suppress the joy of terminating a seventeen-year work relationship. Seventeen years. That was nearly half of my life. I fantasized about how liberated I would soon feel.

The 5 p.m. conversation on that Friday did not go the way I expected.

It was a business-as-usual meeting. I received more projects to tackle and things to do. "Is there anything else we need to talk about?" I asked my boss, hopefully, at the end of the meeting.

"Have a good flight" was all I got in response.

My head exploded as I left his office. Instead of liberation, I got perpetuation.

I hated that soul-sucking job. I did not know how I could face another day in that organization. Every morning my stomach churned as I drove to work. I hated the office politics. The "always-on" expectations. The 10 p.m. conference calls. The bureaucracy.

I hated everything about that job *except* for the paycheck. Then I hated myself for not having the guts to walk away from that paycheck. I felt as if I gave a small piece of my heart every time I walked into my very nice office, with its expansive views and modern furniture. I was a wage slave. Trapped. Stuck inside a "good" job at a high-profile company in a sexy industry. I had a decent personal balance sheet, but my assets were unproductive. I did not have independent cash flow. I *depended* upon that salary. Although most other aspects of my life rocked, the unhappiness at work polluted everything else.

An enriched life, this was not.

THE MANY WORK MINDSETS

Think back to last Monday morning.

During your commute into work, what was your frame of mind? Were you looking forward to the day? Or looking forward to the day being over?

If you are lucky, perhaps your thoughts were optimistic…

Financially Secure Mindset: The new project excites me. It could game-change the company and my career. Sure, it's risky, but we have a shot at making a big difference in the market. This opportunity energizes me while I work my butt off to make sure we get it right. If we do not greenlight the project, everything will be okay. I can afford to take a chunk of time off. Heck, I would enjoy some time off. Either way, I win.

Alternatively, were you less upbeat last Monday morning? Perhaps this is more familiar…

Hanging-On Mindset: I need this job. I have a kid in college and another on the way to University. I have years left on my mortgage and I'm years behind in my retirement readiness. I am screwed if the market does not recover. If the rumored restructuring happens, I'm also screwed. I have to suck up to Bob to make sure I will be safe. I can't make any ripples. Gotta make sure I survive this. I need that December bonus.

Or maybe your commuting thoughts last Monday morning were along these lines…

This Sucks Mindset: I hate this job. I cannot believe I missed seeing my son score that goal on Saturday because of that stupid conference call with my boss. I wish Margaret would get a life so everyone else could have one, too. That fire drill last week with the Boston client. What a waste of time. My wife is still pissed that I missed dinner because of that farce. I need a drink already, and it is not even 9 a.m. I hope I can get through this bloody day without losing my mind.

Then there is that other prevalent mindset, the This-Job-Is-Everything Mindset.

My first encounter with this archetype occurred more than two decades ago, and it set off a personal chain reaction. Barely thirty at the time, I noticed a Japanese colleague, whom I will call Watanabe-san, standing forlornly by the window. He vacantly watched the frenzied streets thirty-two floors below. Known as a *lifer* in the company, Watanabe-san had recently learned the company no longer needed his services. He was in his early fifties. His career was over. To Watanabe-san, his career was *everything*.

"What am I going to do now, Todd-san?" he asked me. "I've worked for this company for my entire life. What else is there?"

I understood my colleague's sense of nihilism entirely. Not long before, I also had a work crisis, one that shook me to the core and turned my views about work and life upside down.

It was my first job out of Columbia Business School. My dream job working for a Hollywood studio. Back then, I often laughed on paydays. It seemed outrageous to earn money from doing something I found so exciting and personally rewarding.

Then I tumbled.

I negotiated a deal with a Taiwanese company. The agreement was so important that the division president directly called me for updates. Closing this one deal would be my moment to shine.

So, what did I do? I did what any ambitious, newly minted MBA would do. I negotiated aggressively to prove myself. Too aggressively, it turned out. At 6 p.m. on a Friday, I received a terse message that said, "Thank you for your efforts, but the gap is too big. The deal is off."

F@%#!

I scrambled through a flurry of desperate calls to my counterpart on the other side of the negotiation. It was too late. The weekend had officially begun, and this was before the age of cell phones. Reaching the client over the weekend would prove impossible. The only thing I could do was wait for a miserable Monday morning.

That weekend was excruciating. I couldn't sleep or function. I only could replay the negotiation repeatedly in my head, each time blowing the deal even more spectacularly. Why had I pushed so hard on a deal that I could not afford to lose? That weekend I sat motionless on my living room floor, propped against the couch, staring blankly at a white wall. The *shame* of blowing this deal was almost unbearable.

Sixty very dark hours later, Monday morning arrived, and so did a second chance. I groveled to the client and salvaged the deal.

Surviving that painful experience changed me, personally and professionally.

I quickly realized that the transactions would only get bigger and the stakes higher as I progressed in my career. To maintain sanity, I needed to develop a concrete system for staying grounded when things fell apart at work, as surely they would. I needed a mechanism to keep perspective on what is most important.

I resolved never to allow work to define my self-worth and Identity. I would not defer the things that fire me up. I would not accept the default setting. A thriving career was no longer adequate. I demanded an enriched life.

I would be ready for the guy at a cocktail party who asks, so *what do you do?*

But that was not enough. As focused as I was on life goals, back then I failed to appreciate the importance of accelerating financial security. I was a rising star at work and quickly climbing the corporate ladder. At the time, I loved my job and my company. Financial security never even crossed my mind.

A decade later, financial *in*security handicapped me, and I realized that economic security is foundational. Upon this realization, I hustled to fast-track financial freedom.

Less than five years later, using the principles in this book, I achieved outright financial security. I was no longer a wage slave. Though I continued to work for several more years, employment became optional. When you *choose* to work, you *anticipate* Monday mornings.

Over the years, I have encountered many versions of Watanabe-san, many Hangers-On, and many This Sucks types. These are frequently recurring characters in the corporate world. Among the independently employed, variations of these archetypes also abound. Sometimes the corporate executive gets the wrong end of a restructuring, or a high-flying career hits a speed bump. Sometimes the workaholic lawyer burns out chasing billable hours, or the stay-at-home mom confronts an empty nest. Sometimes the consultant bows to clients, or the entrepreneur faces fundraising headwinds.

The triggers vary, but the problems are universal. Each of these people has a sense of incompleteness and imbalance—a lack of control.

Perhaps you know one of these archetypes. Maybe one of these Monday morning mindsets is uncomfortably close to home?

THE MISERY MALAISE

"You have to realize," an accomplished attorney said over after-work cocktails, in between gulps of sherry and soda, "that 99 percent of these people are miserable. Look around you," she wryly remarked as we surveyed the packed lounge. "They have all the money in the world. They have everything they think they are supposed to want. And they hate their lives."

Ninety-nine percent may be a stretch. But in high-octane cities where the professional elite tends to congregate—places like New York, Los Angeles, and Hong Kong—it certainly *seems* like 99 percent are miserable. Want proof? Just observe the facial expressions in any elevator lobby of any prime office building in any major city on any Monday morning.

Objectively, across so many metrics, this is a great time to be alive. We should enjoy life and enjoy each other. Yet the opposite happens. There is a white-collar misery epidemic. "It's official," screamed a headline in the UK newspaper *The Telegraph*. "Most people are miserable at work."

The reality of modern professional life, chasing that elusive carrot, looks something like this:

"The trouble with being in a rat race," quipped the comedian, Lily Tomlin, "is that even if you win the race, you're still a rat."

We go to the right schools, follow the rules, and pay our dues. After working so hard to climb the ladder of success, what a disappointment when we find the ladder leans against the wrong wall, to paraphrase Thomas Merton. Worse, we spend so much time building career skills, we forget to build life skills. We discover we can adeptly manage businesses but often suck when it comes to managing a personal account, advancing personal goals, and protecting non-work time.

This creates job disengagement, a deep detachment from work. Nationally, about one-third of all workers disengage, and a majority wish they were working somewhere else. A 2018 Gallup study found that, at all levels, nearly 25 percent of employees feel burned out at work very often if not always.

This malaise has three root causes:

1. Financial Insecurity
2. Time Poverty
3. Stalled Progress Toward Personal Priorities

1. FINANCIAL INSECURITY

November 2019 was a blissful economic time; US unemployment was at a record low and the stock markets were at record highs. Yet, according to the US Financial Health Pulse 2019 Trends Report, only 29 percent of Americans were financially healthy. Put another way, even under almost perfect economic conditions, seven out of ten adult Americans were either "financially coping" or "financially vulnerable." Financial insecurity persists even among high earners, who typically have expensive cost structures to accompany high salaries.

Most people equate financial security with job security. That is dangerous. Job security can diminish at all levels—including those precious white-collar jobs—because of unprecedented world events (such as the coronavirus recession) and accelerations in technological disruption, globalization, corporate consolidation, and outsourcing. "A job—once the guarantor of income security— no longer reliably plays that role," declares *The New York Times*. Simply look at the times we are living in now. The COVID-19 pandemic walloped the economy and caused an unemployment epidemic. In April 2020, in the pandemic aftermath, US job losses went off the charts, with *just 51 percent of adult Americans* occupying full-time jobs. Dependency upon a paycheck, especially a tenuous paycheck, creates a zero-sum situation. That is never a happy place to be.

2. TIME POVERTY

Time poverty is the second root cause of the misery malaise. We manage our personal time like we manage our own money, which is to say, not very well. A global study conducted in eight countries by Ernst & Young found that insufficient time accounts for four of the five biggest hurdles professionals face:

- Getting enough sleep
- "Finding time for me"
- "Finding time for family and friends"
- Additional hours worked

Many professionals feel overscheduled, overextended, overloaded, and overwhelmed. Attention spans have declined since the mobile revolution. The average attention span now lasts eight seconds, which is less than the attention span of a goldfish. Through multitasking, we somehow squeeze thirty-one hours of activity into a twenty-four-hour day.

No wonder we feel life is out of control.

For many people, a massive gap exists between how we spend our days, and how we want to spend our days. The paradox of wealth: We make more money, but not more time. For many, earning money takes less effort than gaining time.

3. STALLED PROGRESS TOWARD PERSONAL PRIORITIES

Priorities is the third root cause of the malaise. Not stalled career progress, but hampered advancement toward long-term, salient personal goals.

Take New Year's resolutions as an example. These are inherently personal and conceived to take inventory. Rarely on New Year's Eve do we pledge work goals. This is a private moment to commit, or recommit, to whatever we think will improve our well-being in the coming year. It does not take long to abandon these personal goals. According to *US News & World Report*, 80 percent of us fail to achieve our New Year's resolutions; most people quit within six weeks of starting.

This malaise might affect women even more. In December 2019, women held the majority of jobs in the US. Working women extend hours in the office without reducing domestic responsibilities, reports *The Wall Street Journal*. As a result, women shortchange sleep, socializing, and relaxation.

Sometimes this misery malaise causes acute symptoms, such as my state-of-mind during my final months at the Hollywood studio, when I was eager to be fired. But more commonly, the problem manifests as negative sentiments such as unhappiness, stress, frustration, fear, anger, loneliness, apathy, or even helplessness. These dispiriting emotions drain energy and suck the life out of life.

Enough about the problem. This book provides strategies to help you reclaim and enrich your life.

THE SOLUTION

The Oxford English Dictionary says to enrich is to:

⑤ Improve or enhance the quality or value of
⑤ Make (someone) wealthy or wealthier

The ENRICH methodology delivers this. Through a six-step process, ENRICH teaches you how to accelerate financial security, create time wealth, and Ignite what's most important. In short, this book empowers you to create the *life you really want*. The progress you make day-to-day and month-to-month may be incremental. The cumulative impact of these strategies transforms.

ESSENTIALIZE **E**   NARROW **N**   REACH **R**   IGNITE **I**   CALIBRATE **C**   HARNESS TIME **H**

Step I: Essentialize. The first step addresses that tasty question—what makes life delicious?

Step II: Narrow. Prioritize your priorities. Avoid the default setting. If you do not define your priorities, someone else will.

Step III: Reach. An enriched life does not happen accidentally. It requires setting compelling goals and relentless Intentionality to get to where you want to go. This step is the heart of ENRICH. You'll create a Life Plan and build Annual Financial Plans. You'll also learn how to future-proof your finances and reverse the financial paradigm. Hint: work *your* money, rather than work *for* money.

Step IV: Ignite. Convert your plans to reality with actionable strategies to get going, maintain momentum, and overcome fear.

Step V: Calibrate. Enhance life's deliciousness, at work and home.

Step VI: Harness Time. When you control your time, you control your life.

These six steps evolve from theorizing to goal setting to planning to doing. To put action to these core strategies, ENRICH presents an extensive tool kit with more than eighty tactics. Eleven "Take Action" exercises help put these principles into practice. Appendices I and II contain cheat sheet summaries of all these tools and tactics.

Finally, a couple of caveats about this method: the process takes commitment and hard work. "There are no shortcuts to any place worth going," the soprano Beverly Sills said fondly. Also, be ready to stretch your mind, as some of the strategies challenge mainstream convictions, and quite possibly your own.

ENRICH: KEY TAKEAWAYS: MONDAY MORNING MALAISE

Chasing that elusive carrot is the default setting for many professionals. Just because seemingly 99 percent of the professional population is miserable does not mean you must be. Your mindset on Monday mornings and the overall quality of your life reflect your choices. There is a viable and empowering alternative to the misery malaise.

- The Monday Morning Malaise is real—and common.
- This unhappiness stems from financial insecurity, time poverty, and a disconnect with what's most important.
- ENRICH empowers you to create the life you want.

We're ready for the first ENRICH step. In the next chapter, we encounter the concept of "Essentialize"—to savor the ingredients that make life delicious. I'll go over eight "Essentials" and present some convincing research about what enriches life.

ESSENTIALIZE

What inflates life?

Which is more valuable: money or time?

How does pistachio shrapnel fit into the picture?

(What the hell is pistachio shrapnel, anyway?)

On this journey together, our ultimate goal is to create time wealth, financial security, and Ignite what's most important. To get there, the first step is to "Essentialize." This means to inject into our lifestyles the essential ingredients that make life delicious.

Nicholas Epley, a Behavioral Science professor at the University of Chicago, says happiness is not a permanent state. Epley compares happiness to a leaky tire. We have to pump air into a tire from time to time to keep it inflated. Similarly, we need to regularly infuse our lives with the ingredients that elate and enrich.

ESSENTIALIZE **E** NARROW **N** REACH **R** IGNITE **I** CALIBRATE **C** HARNESS TIME **H**

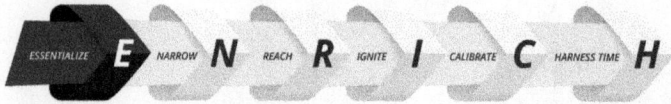

Chapter 2 introduces the eight Essentials and explains how they enrich. In this chapter, we also consider a childhood education, take a personal inventory, and address a ubiquitous pain point among professionals—the time vs. money conundrum.

CHAPTER 2

THE ESSENTIAL EIGHT

"Never get so busy making a living that you forget to make a life. "
—DOLLY PARTON

"Life moves pretty fast. If you don't stop and look around once in a while, you could miss it."
—FERRIS BUELLER IN THE 1986 FILM, *FERRIS BUELLER'S DAY OFF*

California pistachios saved Danny Burke's life.

Cleaning an outside window of his tenth floor Hong Kong apartment, British-born Burke tumbled. One hundred feet and 2.4 terrifying seconds later—as calculated by his mathematician father—he crashed on a pile of industrial-sized pistachio bags. Wearing only boxer shorts, pistachio "shrapnel" punctured his near-naked body. But shells from the power punch nut were the least of Burke's issues. The collision with that heap of pistachios shaved his scalp back two inches, exposing his skull. The impact dislocated his arm and shoulder and fractured his C7 vertebra. His right hand was engorged to three times the size of his left.

As Burke explains to me some months later, in between enthusiastic bites of chicken wings:

> What went through my head that moment, when I realized I lost control, is I am going to die. This is it. Ten floors meant inevitable death. I did not see how it could be any other way. My next vision was multicolored plastics. It made no sense. I thought I was in some afterworld and was so confused. I thought I was in a plastic Hell. In an afterworld, you would think there is something resembling nature. With so much plastic, I thought I had fucked up in a bad way. Then in my peripheral vision, I see a Chinese face. I realized neurologically I am OK. I had landed on a 1.4 sq. meter pallet of California pistachio nuts. Lifesaving qualities in those nuts!

Six weeks after the accident, with urgency and fearlessness, Burke ran down a Balinese volcano wearing a thoracic brace. That little inconvenience did not stop him from fully embracing life. As he tells me with gusto:

> After an accident like that, you go into survival mode. The emotions catch up later. After three weeks, I was crying every day. Tears were mainly out of joy. It's an appreciation of being alive.

The accident emphasized what he already knew: "Time is the most precious asset." Burke had always felt "caged" in the office. Even before the accident, he eschewed the usual 5-2 ratio of workdays to weekends. "I didn't want to put dreams on hold and have life pass by," Burke explains. After traveling nomadically around the world for five years, he decided to anchor. That led him to the tenth-floor apartment.

> After the fall, I had an incredible drive. It was like a Matchbox

car when you pull it back. So much kinetic energy. The accident cut out the bullshit. Caring what other people think has been removed. This second lease on life emphasizes what you want to do, and you just do it. I used to be a procrastinator. Now I realize we only have a certain amount of time. In many ways, my path has not changed, but it did change my perspective. I cherish relationships and friendships.

Falling out of a tenth-floor window provided a clarifying moment for Danny Burke. This near-death plunge gave him an acute appreciation of time, and an urgency to live *intentionally*. Refusing to squander this second chance, Burke savors life.

But what makes life worth savoring? What makes it satisfying and delicious? In other words, what are the factors that contribute to an enriched form of living?

A CHILDHOOD EDUCATION

Try this: Imagine a period when your life was sweet and carefree. If you are lucky, perhaps that period was childhood. If so, picture as vividly as possible, the details of a blissful childhood. How the days were filled with activity. The abundance of friends and family. The smiles, the laughter. The ways kids embrace everything the world offers and then some.

Beyond the apparent absence of worries and pressures, several factors make childhood such an ideal period:

- Social connections are abundant, tight, and easy to forge. Making new friends happens frequently and naturally.
- Kids are insatiably curious, trying to figure out how the world works.

- Meals are balanced and healthy (broccoli be damned), rest is plentiful, and hours and hours of physical and outdoor activity fill the day, all while basking in the warmth of family relationships.
- Kids have the ultimate financial security (their parents!) and absolute clarity on their Identity. Many children are proud to be themselves and are not interested in being anyone else or anywhere else. They focus on the here and now and do not preoccupy themselves with accomplishment. They celebrate milestones, however big or small.
- Most children do not expect too much from the world. They feel content with what they find.

All these happy qualities are uniquely tied to that special time of life we call childhood. Eventually, even for those blessed with perfect childhoods, life happens. As responsibilities accumulate, we begin to sacrifice those valuable intangibles—physical activity, the ease of making new friends, exploring curiosities. Life quickly gets complicated. The world expects more from you, and you expect more from it.

Does it have to be like that? Do these qualities have to elude us as we grow older? Or might an enriched adult life replicate the same characteristics that make childhood blissful?

LIFE SUCCESS FACTORS

I have spent decades keenly observing individuals like Danny Burke—individuals who grab life by the cajones and run with it, even if they're wearing a thoracic brace. These are individuals who consistently crush it. They've managed to maintain in adulthood the fulfillment most of us experienced in childhood. What life success factors do they have in common?

Combining my observations of these individuals with research from the science of happiness, I've distilled life success to eight factors. I call these the eight "Essentials." These are the intangible elements that make life satisfying and delicious. Here's how I refined these eight ingredients.

Numerous factors influence well-being, but let us focus on two highly regarded measures of how people feel about their daily lives:

1. Martin Seligman is the godfather of positive psychology. His theory of well-being consists of five measurable elements, which go by the PERMA acronym: Positive emotion, engagement, (positive) relationships, meaning, and achievement.
2. The Gallop-Sharecare Well-Being Index provides another measure of well-being. This index surveys over 175,000 respondents each year. With more than two million cumulative interviews, it comprises the world's most extensive data set on well-being. This index tracks five factors to measure well-being: Purpose, social, financial, community, and physical.

For the delicious life recipe, synthesize common ingredients between PERMA and the Well-Being Index. Then add some unique flavorings that many professionals consider vital—Identity, Intentionality, and Integration. Together, these eight Essentials make life delicious. These are the building blocks, or DNA, of an enriched life:

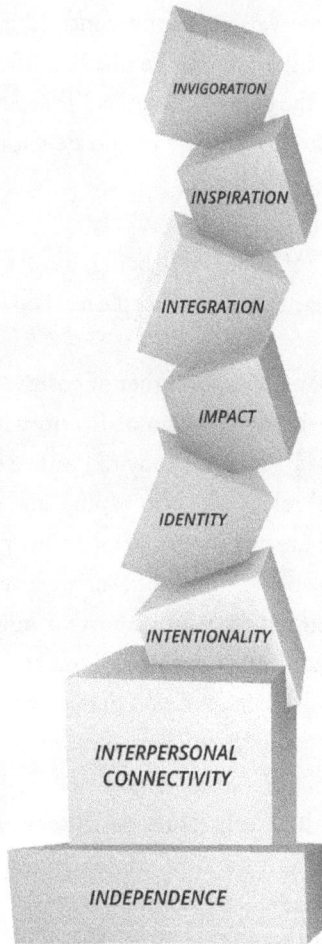

INVIGORATION

INSPIRATION

INTEGRATION

IMPACT

IDENTITY

INTENTIONALITY

INTERPERSONAL CONNECTIVITY

INDEPENDENCE

In my experience and from my observations, having an adequate presence of each Essential drives a sustained and enriched life. We need these elements. They are like vitamins. They are essential, and without them we manifest symptoms of deficiency. It may not be possible or even realistic to experience every element every day, or even every week. But over time, we *feel* their absence. That's when life feels out of control, and those deflating, distracting, draining negative emotions fill the void.

These Essentials purposely begin with the letter "I," representing self. *You* are at the center. These Essentials revolve around *you* and contribute to *your* well-being.

THE EIGHT ESSENTIALS

Let's now unpack the science behind these life success factors, and how each Essential helps to construct an enriched life. This is the theoretical foundation of the ENRICH method. With this understanding, we can turn to the practical aspects of how to lead an enriched life—this involves setting priorities (chapter 3), formulating a Life Plan (chapter 5), and engineering financial security (chapters 6 and 7). We'll tackle integrating the eight Essentials into daily life in "Habits for Enriched Happiness" (chapter 11).

If these Essentials are so important, why wait until chapter 11? Because enriching life is a complex process. There are many interconnected moving parts—personal, financial, and professional. The ENRICH method unifies all these moving parts into a *complete* solution to the Monday Morning Malaise. This process works because it integrates and addresses *all* the aspects of modern professional life, unlike most other self-improvement methods that isolate and focus on a single issue.

To start, let's examine the most significant Essential:

INTERPERSONAL CONNECTIVITY

The Harvard Grant study, initiated during the Great Depression by a Harvard physician helps us answer the primary question about what most enriches life. It asked, how do people adapt to life? This contrasted with contemporary medical research of the time, which tended to focus on the diagnosis and treatment of disease.

Over many years, this longitudinal study looked at an exhaustive range of data points at every life stage. The research probed beyond health and habits to encompass careers, social history, intellectual functioning, personality assessment, and other factors. Thousands of discrete data points tell a holistic story about life success patterns. *The Harvard Gazette* explains:

> Close relationships, more than money or fame, are what keep people happy throughout their lives, the study revealed. Those ties protect people from life's discontents, help to delay mental and physical decline, and are better predictors of long and happy lives than social class, IQ, or even genes...individuals who most connected to their family, friends, community, and other people were the healthiest and happiest.

This decades-long research substantiates something your grandmother probably told you when you were a child. Loving relationships throughout life have the most significant positive impact on life satisfaction. People love you back; your job and gadgets do not. As George Vaillant, who directed the Grant study for more than thirty years, said, "Happiness is love. Full stop."

A meta-study conducted by researchers at Brigham Young University and the University of North Carolina at Chapel Hill reviewed 148 individual studies. These involved more than 300,000 participants and spanned more than a century. The meta-study concluded that the interaction of friends, family, and even colleagues can extend your life. Overall, for adults, robust social networks extend longevity by 50 percent. The benefits of a healthy social life can be as positive as giving up a smoking habit of fifteen cigarettes a day.

So there you have it. Warm relationships contribute the most to an enriched life.

Here's the rub: building community and forging long-lasting relationships demands hard work and time. Many professionals struggle with this. The quality and availability of close friendships often deteriorate as an unintended consequence of financial and professional success. In chapter 11, we will consider some tactics to foster community and build relationships.

INDEPENDENCE

Now let's try to answer that perennial question: does money buy happiness?

There are two currencies of Independence—financial Independence and time Independence. Money gets the most attention. Society prioritizes financial wealth over time wealth and celebrates "more." We often think that a bigger house, longer boat, or faster car is the key to a better life. The pursuit of "more" can be endless and unsatisfying—a "perpetual mode of dissatisfaction," in the words of one professional I interviewed for background research.

When does "more" lead to "more happy?"

The simple answer is: maybe never. Numerous studies indicate that after a certain point, increases in income and wealth do not translate to equal—or any—improvements in life satisfaction. More money doesn't necessarily translate to more happiness. Consider the landmark 2010 study by the Nobel laureate psychologist and economist, Daniel Kahneman. His research, along with Angus Deaton's, identified $75,000 annual income as the inflection point. They distinguished between emotional well-being (joy, stress, anger, affection) and life evaluation (how people think about their life on a scale from "worst possible life" to "best possible life"). Kahneman and Deaton analyzed more than 450,000 responses to the Gallup

Well-Being Index. They found that an individual's emotional well-being peaks at $75,000, but a positive correlation between income and life evaluation continues after that point. "We conclude that high income buys life satisfaction but not happiness, and that low income is associated both with low life evaluation and low emotional well-being," write Kahneman and Deaton.

This study focuses on the United States. In 2018 researchers at Purdue and the University of Virginia looked at income satiation internationally, examining a representative sample of 1.7 million individuals worldwide using Gallup World Poll data. "Globally, we find that satiation occurs at $95,000 for life evaluation," the researchers write in *Nature Human Behavior*. In North America, they found the satiation threshold to be at $105,000—or $115,000 among the highly educated. Here's the kicker: "In certain parts of the world, incomes beyond satiation are associated with lower life evaluations." In other words, more money makes people less happy.

To summarize: if you insist on putting a price tag on it, and you probably do, the income sweet spot lies between $75,000 and $115,000. Anything beyond that has diminishing marginal value. Chapter 6 cites three additional respected studies, each pointing to the same conclusion. To be clear, this concept is qualitative, not quantitative. We do not need as much money as we think.

The second Independence currency is time affluence, which means having sufficient time for what is most important. Time is more valuable than money. Time is scarce, and we value what is rare. You can produce more money, but you cannot manufacture more time.

"What should you choose: Time or Money?" UCLA business school professors, Hal Hershfield and Cassie Mogilner Holmes ask in *The New York Times*. They put this question to more than

4,000 people at different ages and found that most people (64 percent) prioritize money over time. Hershfield and Mogilner observed, "The people who chose time over money were on average statistically happier and more satisfied with life than the people who chose money." After factoring gender, occupation, marital and parental status, the amount of leisure time and how the respondents value material possessions, the research reveals time still trumps money when it comes to happiness. "In our pursuit of happiness," they write,

> We are constantly faced with decisions, both big and small, that force us to pit time against money. Of course, sometimes it's not a choice at all: We must earn that extra pay to make ends meet. But when it is a choice, the likelihood of choosing more time over more money—despite the widespread tendency to do the opposite—is a good sign you'll enjoy the happiness you seek.

Independence anchors an enriched life because accelerating the first currency (financial security) accelerates the second currency (time affluence).

Most "happiness" books ignore financial concerns. They often treat money as a dirty word when considering life's big questions. However, we cannot ignore the fact that money matters, especially for high achievers. Dependency upon a paycheck (that is, the absence of financial security) can lead to miserable Monday mornings. If you worry about income or debt, you feel you have few or no options, regardless of how well the other aspects of your life are going. Financial *insecurity* produces stress and worry, messes with your mind, and can lead to all kinds of suboptimal behaviors and outcomes.

Financial *security*, on the other hand, creates optionality at work and in life and enables you to focus on the things that matter.

This time vs. money trade-off is one of the biggest hurdles we face. "How is the average person supposed to achieve financial Independence and financial security if she doesn't choose money over time first?" a friend asks bluntly.

Rethinking the financial paradigm solves this dilemma. The chapters on accelerating financial security (chapter 6, chapter 7, and chapter 8) dive into this topic.

IDENTITY

Professionals like my former colleague Watanabe-san routinely get stuck in an Identity trap, overestimating the importance of career to life satisfaction. A common sentiment: "A lot of my self-worth was aligned with my professional status," an unemployed forty-something executive confesses to *The New York Times*. In this article about well-connected high earners whose careers are on hold, he continued, "When that changes it's [a] huge blow to ego."

The Australian Bronnie Ware cared for terminally ill patients in the final three to twelve weeks of their lives. After eight years of providing palliative care, she noticed many recurring themes in the thoughts and the regrets of the dying. She summarized these in a viral blog post called *Top Five Regrets of the Dying*, which she later expanded into a memoir. The #1 regret: "I wish I dared to live a life true to myself, not the life others expected of me."[1]

The central lesson from Watanabe-san's predicament is always to define who you are as something higher than work, and your purpose as something larger than self. Identity describes what

---

1   The other four most frequent regrets are: I wish I hadn't worked so hard; I wish I had the courage to express my feelings; I wish I had stayed in touch with my friends; and I wish I had let myself be happier.

you stand for, not what you do. You own your Identity; it does not depend upon anything or anyone else. Crucially, your self-worth also has absolutely nothing to do with your net worth.

The Japanese have a versatile word to describe your purpose in life: *Ikigai*. *Ikigai* separates the Identity of self from the identification of work.

INTENTIONALITY

Ikigai also captures that thing you live for: what gets you out of bed each morning and keeps you going. How you intentionally allocate your time. To live intentionally is to look to the horizon, and deliberately propel yourself toward what gives your life meaning. This is why the forward-looking Life Plan plays a central role in this process.

Intentionality literally gives you a reason to live. *National Geographic* Fellow, Dan Buettner, studies those with extended life spans—the ultimate high achievers. Some societies, like Okinawa, Japan, have exceptional longevity. Admittedly, lifestyle factors, such as exercise and healthy diets, contribute to long life. But there is also something else. Societies with exceptional lifespans are communal. They emphasize healthy social relationships, family and community, and a "cooperative spirit," among other shared traits. Within these communities, individuals have a deep sense of meaning and purpose.

IMPACT

Most professionals aspire to make a difference. We share a desire to engage meaningfully in and with the world. We want to contribute to something bigger, whether at work, at home, at school, or in our community.

Joint researchers in Michigan and Korea have found a strong correlation between meaning and life satisfaction, health, and longevity. More than 700 adult Americans volunteered in this Meaning of Life study. The researchers' clear conclusion: a life framed by purpose satisfies more than a life centered on pleasure.

INTEGRATION

Work-life balance is a source of constant frustration among time-starved professionals. Balance is a binary relationship. If one side is up, the other must be down. Balance is like playing a game of whack-a-mole; you may attain equilibrium momentarily, but it is hard to maintain it long enough to feel complete.

Gandhi described happiness as when "what you think, what you say and what you do are in harmony." Integration harmoniously and seamlessly fuses the personal, professional, and financial. It offers a different way to think about the work-life equation. With Integration, your highest priorities fit together. You feel in control, and accommodate what's most important, including these eight Essentials.

Gratitude and giving back are salient aspects of Integration. Appreciate the whole, not the holes. Regularly expressing thanks and giving back calms, completes, and integrates the various facets of our lives.

INSPIRATION

Inspiration is the secret sauce that makes life delicious.

As careers advance and specialization increases, our intellectual range narrows. Over time, we simply slow down the learning.

Professionals at all levels frequently complain about diminishing intellectual stimulation. When you've done something for the 101st time, no matter how complex, it poses less of a mental challenge.

To maintain mental fitness, we need ongoing inspiration. The novelist, Tom Clancy, gets to the point: "When you stop learning," he said, "you die." There are many reasons why continually enriching your life with inspiration pays off. People who keep learning tend to:

- Earn more
- Live longer
- Enjoy broader and more numerous social circles
- Have more confidence
- Be more interesting

INVIGORATION

Invigoration means fitness, proper nutrition, and healthy living—the things that physically enrich life. Scientists have found that a single session of exercise alters 9,815 molecules in our blood. Invigoration is the closest thing to a magic pill to enhance life.

Ironically, when pressed for time, we often sacrifice this Essential that delivers so much power. The good news: it's free, and you can invigorate almost anywhere.

People often ask me why health is not an Essential. The litmus test is control. There are times when health is beyond your control because of hereditary or environmental factors. On the other hand, your choices influence your physical fitness, nutrition, and lifestyle.

THE ESSENTIALS INVENTORY

Now that we have surveyed the theory and science underlying the eight Essentials, let's bring it home to what matters: you. Take a moment to sit up or stand tall, then take a snapshot of the presence or absence of these Essentials in your life. This inventory will help you identify what might be missing so you can frame your priorities and goals in the coming chapters. To take stock of each Essential, ask yourself the following questions over various periods…today, this week, this month. Honor your gut reactions.

Do you agree that this is an essential ingredient of a delicious life? If you agree, how satisfied are you with this Essential's abundance in your life?

Here are some more questions specific to each Essential.

INTERPERSONAL CONNECTIVITY:

- Are your family and social connections stable?
- Are your relationships warm?
- Whom can you call at 3 a.m.?
- When did you last make a new friend?
- Do the people who surround you lift you up or bring you down?

INDEPENDENCE:

- Do you feel financially secure?
- How much is enough?
- How would you cope with sudden job loss?
- Do you have sufficient resources for an emergency expense?
- Are you on track with long-term financial goals, even if you live to age one hundred?

- Do you have enough time for the people and things that are most important to you?
- Do you feel in control of your schedule and your time?
- Or do you feel that work controls you?

IDENTITY:

- In social situations, how do you introduce yourself?
- How would you most like to describe yourself, or be described?
- How do you define success?
- What do you stand for?
- Do you have an Identity outside work, or is your job title your Identity?

INTENTIONALITY:

- Do you consider how you spend your days as deliberate and purposeful?
- Do you have clear priorities?
- Are you on course to fulfill your aspirations?
- Is how you spend your days consistent with your preferences?

IMPACT:

- Do you contribute to something bigger?
- Does your output make a difference?
- When did you last accomplish something significant?
- Does a "joy" factor exist in your career, or does your job feel like hard work?

INTEGRATION:

- Do you feel pulled in different directions?

- Are your responsibilities and activities harmonious, cohesive, and whole?
- Or are they disjointed, unbalanced, and unsteady?
- Do you focus on the whole or the holes?
- Do you express gratitude and routinely give back as much as you can (or should)?

INSPIRATION:

- Do you immerse yourself in people, ideas, places, and works of art that give you energy and spark joy?
- Do you routinely experience or cultivate wonder, curiosity, or spirituality?
- When did you last learn something new, or try something new?
- Do you regularly feel stimulated emotionally and intellectually?
- Do you periodically encounter fresh ideas outside of your professional orbit?

INVIGORATION:

- Are you satisfied with your health and fitness?
- Are you satisfied with the quality of your nutrition?
- How often do you break a sweat?
- Do you get adequate rest?
- When did you last enjoy the outdoors?
- When was your last proper vacation?

What does this inventory reveal? Which Essentials are charged fully in your life? Which need nourishment? Which are missing altogether?

ENRICH: KEY TAKEAWAYS: THE ESSENTIAL EIGHT

In his memoir, the pioneering Swiss psychiatrist and champion of "true self," Carl Jung, observes:

> [I] have frequently seen people become neurotic when they content themselves with inadequate or wrong answers to the questions of life. They seek position, marriage, reputation, outward success or money, and remain unhappy and neurotic even when they have attained what they were seeking. Such people are usually contained within too narrow a spiritual horizon. Their life has not sufficient content, sufficient meaning.

A blissful childhood gives a useful glimpse at how an enriched life might feel, look, and taste. Sometimes a clarifying life event, such as Danny Burke's freefall from his apartment window, creates an acute appreciation of time and an urgency to live intentionally. Other times, we need to take matters into our own hands.

And so, the first ENRICH step is to Essentialize—to activate the Essential ingredients that inflate life and make it delicious. Together, these elements are life's success factors, the building blocks that enrich life. We will further explore how to weave these Essentials into your daily life in chapter 11, Habits for Enriched Happiness.

THE ESSENTIAL EIGHT:

- Interpersonal connectivity plays the most significant, longest-lasting role in life satisfaction.
- Independence anchors us by accelerating financial security and enabling time wealth. Time is the most valuable currency.
- Identity, not your work or net worth, reflects who you truly are.
- Intentionality propels you forward.

- ⑤ Impact provides meaning.
- ⑤ Integration fuses the personal, professional, and financial into a cohesive whole, accommodating what's most important.
- ⑤ Inspiration maintains mental fitness.
- ⑤ Invigoration physically enriches life.

Now that we've explored the eight Essentials, let's progress to the next step: "Narrow"—understanding what's most important to you so you can teach yourself to avoid the default setting.

NARROW

Where do you plug in?

How to avoid your default setting?

What are your nonnegotiables?

"Life is a matter of choices," the leadership maven, John C. Maxwell, suggests, "and every choice you make makes you." The next ENRICH step, Narrow, helps us make the right choices, big and small. If you do not determine your priorities, and by extension your choices, someone or something else will.

Narrowing helps you identify the "core" of the enriched life you will build. This allows you to make choices that reflect what's relatively important.

ESSENTIALIZE **E** NARROW **N** REACH **R** IGNITE **I** CALIBRATE **C** HARNESS TIME **H**

Chapter 3 explains how the default setting gets set. This chapter also introduces two tools—the Mission Statement and the Hierarchy of Priorities—that direct your focus and energy toward what's most important.

CHAPTER 3

AVOID THE DEFAULT SETTING

"Twenty years from now you'll be more disappointed by the things you didn't do than by the ones you did do."

—MARK TWAIN

"Remembering that I'll be dead soon is the most important tool I've ever encountered to help me make the big choices in life. Because almost everything—all external expectations, all pride, all fear of embarrassment or failure—these things just fall away in the face of death, leaving only what is truly important."

—STEVE JOBS

If you could do anything in the world right now, what would you do? More importantly, would you continue doing the work you currently do?

Charles Scott wrestled with these questions. His problem was not that he *didn't* know how he wanted to spend his time—that was clear to him. The challenge lay in reconciling that ideal with the career ladder he felt compelled to climb.

In his career prime at age forty-three, Scott walked away from a fourteen-year tenure with Intel Corporation and an international role in the company's venture capital arm. He'd done well at the world's largest semiconductor chipmaker. He'd flown all over the globe looking for promising investment deals and often interacted directly with Intel's CEO. But the multi-week international business trips had taken a toll on his family life. He wanted more time with his then-young kids and more adventures outside the office. Scott shifted gears and walked away.

Based in New York City, post-Intel Scott was unsure how his career and business model would evolve. He jumped into the deep end to take 100 percent control of his time. Combining two passions, he restyled himself as "the family adventure guy." He cycled over 7,000 miles with his kids—Japan, Iceland, Western Europe, and the Lewis & Clark Trail—over five years.[2]

Scott published two books about these expeditions. However, he realized that writing expedition books would not sustain his family financially. So he dug deep to identify his strengths, his interests, and how he could make a meaningful professional Impact. That process of self-discovery led him to a career as an executive mentor.

He now spends his time speaking and running workshops, in person and virtually, for executives on the topic of "What Do You Want to Be When You Grow Up?" He organizes annual Mastermind Retreat weekends and conducts web sessions with groups of executives. These web sessions take up an hour of his time per week, plus some administrative time, over an eight-week course. This structure allows him to maximize free time *and* maximize

---

2   Upon completion of the Japanese journey, his son officially became the youngest person in history to cycle the length of Japan.

his earnings per hour of work. Helping other executives also gives Scott tremendous professional satisfaction.

I know Scott well; we were roommates at Vanderbilt, and we both jumped off the corporate ladder around the same time a decade ago. Scott stayed off the ladder; I later climbed back on. These days he is hard to track down, because he is all over the map doing the things that light him up, from scaling Mt. Kilimanjaro to running across the Grand Canyon. He also co-founded the charity Team See Possibilities, which enriches the lives of blind children around the world.

I once asked Scott about his proudest achievement at Intel. He paused, looked upward, and then, after some reflection, replied, "The courage to leave."

The courage to leave. Charles Scott exemplifies the one who rejects the default setting.

THE DEFAULT SETTING

Most of us reading this would say that Scott is living the dream. Our lives do not look like his. Instead, we are preconditioned to climb the ladder, without considering alternatives. The typical life arc looks something like this: we spend the first quarter of our lives learning. We then spend roughly half our lives—for many, that's forty years!—earning. In the final quartile of our lives, we then do what we wish we could have done all along. How crazy is this?

The thing is, that was Scott's life arc as well. He was *on* that default path. And it was good to him. It would have been easy for Scott to continue in a comfortable corporate role. Professionally he thrived—he was a success by any standard. But professional success was not enough. He dared to walk away.

How can we have a life that's more like Scott's?

Courage is part of it, of course. But Scott also took control. He managed to reject the default setting by *creating* a viable and superior alternative. He took the time to understand his priorities and then focused on building his life around them.

It wasn't always easy. Economically, it was a difficult journey for Scott to get from the cushy corporate job to where he is now. He went through a challenging period, which he calls "The Abyss," when he burnt through his savings and went into debt. His wife worked at the time but living in Manhattan requires dual incomes. During his career transition, Scott had resolved not to compromise his family's standard of living. This was a nonnegotiable priority.

During The Abyss, Scott thought about returning to the corporate world. Not because he wanted to, but because that was the surest path to supporting his family. But Scott had outlined his priorities and the life he wanted to live; he knew that getting another corporate job would mean failure. So he set an ambitious goal to earn a specific amount of money within a particular time. With the laser clarity of this focus, Scott was able to achieve that goal in six weeks, which led to the next target. He had momentum.

He prospers more today than during his corporate days and enjoys 100 percent control over his time. He figured out how to make money in minimal time and while making a difference in people's lives. "I have become clear on my Hierarchy of Priorities, and allocate my time accordingly," he explains during one late-night conversation. "It does not feel like work," he adds, and he plans to continue doing this for the rest of his life.

Many of us accept the default setting because it's easier and there's little resistance. With life set on default, someone or something else usually dictates how we spend our time. Professionals, even the most senior, must react to time pressures imposed by a boss, a client, a constituent, or a market situation. For many professionals, a few of whom I interviewed for this book, the most significant measure of success is not their bank balance. It is whether they have 100 percent control over their time.

Reaching for that kind of control and time freedom can be petrifying—assuming we even know what we want. Often, we don't know what we want because we haven't invested the time to consider the possibilities. And so we sometimes knowingly stay on the default setting because the alternative is too uncomfortable. Reacting to someone else's agenda can be simpler than working with self-awareness. Responding to someone else's deadlines and priorities means we do not have to create our own. Accepting the default setting permits a convenient cop-out.

That does not lead to an enriched life. In this chapter, we'll explore how you can find what truly matters to you and begin to build a life around it. This step of "Narrow" helps you identify the core of the life you will create. To start, we'll dissect the thinking behind two tools that can help you narrow priorities: the Mission Statement and your Hierarchy of Priorities.

THE MISSION STATEMENT

When I was an executive at a Hollywood studio, the CEO organized an off-site at the Four Seasons Hotel in Beverly Hills for about a hundred of the studio's most senior executives. The straightforward purpose: to construct a Mission Statement for the company.

This fascinated me. With some roots going back to the 1920s, the studio is hardly a startup. Throughout that time at the Four Seasons, I speculated about the opportunity cost of diverting so much precious executive time to discussing something that seemed academic at best.

The CEO framed the issue this way. The more things change, the more you need to know what you stand for. In the mid-2000s, Hollywood's business model began to fall apart. The CEO assembled this group for two days to discuss, debate, and define a single sentence.

Over the years, I have thought a lot about that experience. The more things change, the more complicated the world gets, the more you need to know your Mission. Companies need Mission Statements to define themselves and their direction.

We need them too.

A durable Mission Statement concisely and explicitly declares who you are and stands the test of time. It encapsulates your life purpose, embodying a long-term vision (where you go) and personal values (who you are).

An effective Mission Statement transcends any one goal or situation. It serves as your compass and facilitates decision-making when you encounter forks in the road. Individuals, couples, and families can create Mission Statements.

Walt Disney's Mission was "to make people happy," and whether in theme parks or film, Disney honored that intent. Let's take some other high-profile examples. Oprah Winfrey aspires "to be a teacher. And to be known for inspiring my students to be more than they thought they could be." That pretty much sums up the effect of her eponymous television show and magazine. Guess whose Mission is "to have fun in [my] journey through life and learn from [my] mistakes?" Sir Richard Branson, the adventurer and Virgin entrepreneur.

What do you stand for? What is sacred? What legacy will you leave? Where do you plug in?

These penetrating questions get to the heart of a Mission Statement.

Above all else, what's most important *to you?* The Take Action exercise at the end of this chapter will help articulate *your* Mission. As Walt Disney said, "It's not hard to make decisions when you know what your values are." Once you develop your Mission Statement, it will become your North Star and guide you in choosing paths that lead you to an enriched life.

However, a Mission Statement alone is not enough. You need to know what's important. You need a Hierarchy of Priorities to understand what matters *more* and what matters *most*.

HIERARCHY OF PRIORITIES

Life is all about the choices we make—big decisions like parenthood or promotion, or small decisions like the gym or an extra hour of sleep. Without a Hierarchy of Priorities, you can find yourself living a life you didn't ask for, driven by default settings, habits, and routines. You can feel overwhelmed by all the "important" stuff demanding your attention. Time can escape you.

This hierarchy keeps you on track by segmenting priorities based on their *relative* importance.

Let me offer a real-world illustration. My partner and I always knew we wanted to become parents. As an adoptee myself, becoming a parent through adoption was essential. For us, parenthood was only a matter of when, not how or what.

Based on our hierarchy system, we considered parenthood a "nonnegotiable," but viewed it as an opaque future event. We were youngish, and our careers were going well. There was no urgency to parenthood.

September 11 changed that. At the end of 2002, we were in New York, our first trip to the city since 9/11. For New Year's Eve we attended a party at a swanky apartment in lower Manhattan, overlooking the former World Trade Center site. Late at night, giant spotlights lit the crater where the Twin Towers once stood. The haunting image of that enormous cavity in lower Manhattan and the impermanence of those iconic buildings stirred me. If the Twin Towers can fall, what does that mean for the rest of us? Life is just too damn short.

Seeing that crater triggered an urgency to pursue our most sacred nonnegotiable priority. Shortly before midnight, with Khaled's Arabesque thumping in the background, I told my partner, "THIS IS THE YEAR." You betcha that was one New Year's resolution we kept.

Our beloved son was born on December 1, 2003.

The rigor of adopting a child in a foreign country bends the mind; it is the administrative equivalent of moving a mountain. There are no accidental adoptions. The complicated and lengthy process by its design weeds people out.

Back then, I juggled two occupations—my day job as a TV executive and my night job as a determined adoptive parent. I went home after work most weeknights and spent hours researching how to accomplish an international adoption. It required unlimited perseverance.

Then the universe tested our resolve. The week we were to fly to meet our infant son and formally kick-start the adoption process, I first had to go to Los Angeles. I had the chance for a big promotion. The only catch was, the new job required relocation to Hong Kong. My partner and I knew that relocating would restart the whole adoption process in a new legal jurisdiction. Realistically, considering the demands of a new job and resettling in a different country, we knew this would delay parenthood by at least a couple of years. It also might permanently jeopardize parenthood.

We confronted a hard and raw decision familiar to many professionals: parenthood or promotion. It was a fork-in-the-road moment. Either way, the course of our lives would dramatically change. Because we knew our priorities, the answer to that gut-wrenching decision was obvious. Paraphrasing Walt Disney, if you know what supersedes everything else, the hard choices become easy. We chose parenthood. Much to our surprise, I still got the promotion. The company graciously allowed me to defer the relocation until after the adoption finalized.

It's not that the job didn't matter to us—it's just that parenthood mattered *more*. The Hierarchy clarified this *relative* importance. (And in the end, we found we could have both.)

PRIORITIZATION PROCESS

Think about all the things that matter to you. Perhaps some combination of family, friends, love, health, wealth, career, faith, self-development, giving back, travel, culture, education, and humanity. How to prioritize these priorities? For most, this is an iterative and long-term process, the work of a lifetime. Your preferences will evolve, dynamically ordering from your nonnegotiables to your nice-to-haves. But it's important to begin the prioritization process *now*, and then review, review, review.

The process to identify what reigns in importance involves brutal honesty, self-awareness, and some tough decisions. You need to hack at branches to get to the roots. For example, if you highly value your career, what precisely about the job do you value? The money, status, responsibilities, or power? Or something else? Ask yourself, "Why?" Then ask "Why" once again. Why is that important? Ask yourself, "Why" again and again. Probe Why, Why, Why to get to the root of an issue.

Consider a lifetime of possibilities. What do you most wish to accomplish, contribute, and experience?

PRIORITIZATION TECHNIQUES

There are several ways to determine your Hierarchy of Priorities. The method I have used for more than two decades involves classifying priorities into four categories:

NONNEGOTIABLE PRIORITIES

IMPORTANT NOW PRIORITIES

IMPORTANT LATER PRIORITIES

NICE-TO-HAVE PRIORITIES

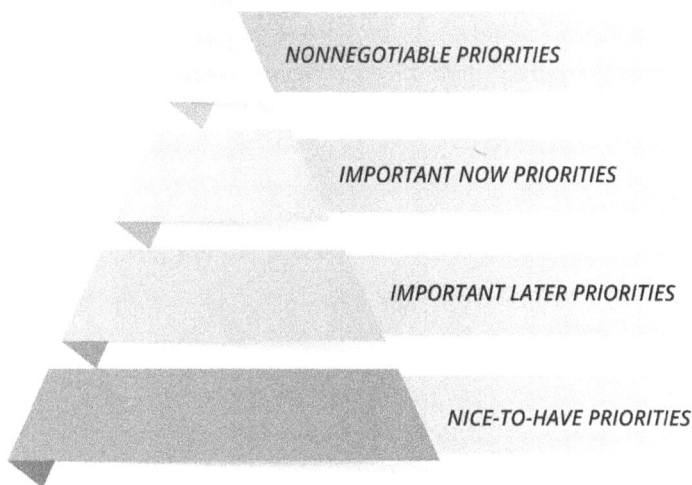

This technique works for me because there's a time element baked into the prioritization. As time evolves, the relative importance of priorities also evolves, up or down, in the ranking. However, it is improbable that the relative importance of your nonnegotiable priorities will change. That is why they are nonnegotiable. Priorities for the next year may look different from priorities for the next five years. But the nonnegotiables should remain constant.

Another approach to prioritization is the so-called ABC method. Similar to my practice, it classifies priorities into three categories. "A" priorities are on top. "B" priorities are secondary. "C" priorities are on the bottom. If you use this method, forget about the "C" priorities and focus on the primary and secondary categories.

A final approach to determine your Hierarchy of Priorities revolves around some advice the billionaire, Warren Buffett, famously gave to his pilot. Buffett reportedly told him to make a list of the Top Twenty-Five things he strove to accomplish in life, and then circle the top five priorities. Later, the pilot showed Buffett the list of twenty-five items. Buffett advised the pilot to focus on the top five and *avoid at all costs* the other twenty until he'd achieved the top five. "Avoid the distractions," Buffett counseled.

Choose a method that feels right to you, stick with it, and formulate your Hierarchy of Priorities.

THE LONG VIEW

When confronted with two competing priorities, ask yourself, *"Which will matter a year from now? Five years from now?"* Use the test of time to determine importance. Often, things that loom large now will be inconsequential in a year.

This hit home during a hot yoga class. Have you ever tried a delicate balancing pose while looking straight up or straight down? It disorients. "To balance, look forward," the yoga teacher advised my wobbly and sweaty class as we attempted the one-legged pose.

Looking far into the future reveals absolute priorities. Zooming out, or viewing the forest rather than the trees, alters relative importance. A change of perspective or time can completely change the picture. To see the big picture, shift your vantage point. Ask what will matter five or ten years from now. Issues or concerns that magnify disproportionately in the present may lose importance over time.

A lifetime is the relevant time horizon to determine nonnegotiable priorities. Real priorities stand the test of time.

HOW TO AVOID THE DEFAULT SETTING

To avoid the default setting, you have to know what carries the highest importance and act upon this awareness. Like I said, if you do not set your priorities, someone else will. Expending valuable time and energy on low priorities, at the expense of higher ones, causes despair and distress among busy individuals.

How many times have you skipped a workout or a family meal because of a work deadline or conference call? Professionals often make these types of daily bargains. The risk is, if you skip today, skipping tomorrow gets easier. The downward slope is slippery.

We don't just bargain with the small things, like meals or gym sessions. We often make grand bargains, too. How many times have we postponed saving a bit more until we get the next promotion? Or taking that family vacation next year instead of now?

Of course, knowing your priorities does not mitigate the demands of a boss or a client. However, understanding your Mission and what is most important does help. This self-awareness gives you a tactical advantage if you act upon it.

To avoid the default setting:

1. Take Care of a Personal Priority First
2. Do Not Delay the Nonnegotiables
3. Make Peace

1. TAKE CARE OF A PERSONAL PRIORITY FIRST

The guaranteed way to act on your aspirations is to tackle one personal goal each day before you cater to anyone else's demands. Think about pre-takeoff safety announcements on an aircraft. In the event of an emergency, the safety advice is to secure your own oxygen mask before helping others. You can better take care of others *after* you take care of yourself. This is not selfish; it is pragmatic.

The priority you start the day with could be progressing toward a personal goal, exercising, or just a few minutes of meditation. Anything. Starting your day by accomplishing something personally important will give you a bounce and feeling of satisfaction that carries you throughout the day. It also takes some sting out of your boss or client's demands. On the other hand, if you leave this personal goal to the end of the day, chances are it will get crowded out. That is how you get stuck on the default setting.

Best of all, tackling a personal priority each day gets you closer to your bigger goals—even with minimal daily progress.

2. DO NOT DELAY THE NONNEGOTIABLES

A sense of disconnect with long-term goals contributes big time to the Monday Morning Malaise, especially if the disconnect occurs with nonnegotiable priorities. If we do not progress toward what we deem personally significant, life feels out of control.

Rarely does a perfect time exist. Is it ever the ideal time to have a baby, save more money, or do anything hard and monumental? Of course not. Waiting for ideal conditions is often just a convenient excuse.

Continuing with the parenting example: if creating a family is a nonnegotiable priority, is "now is not a good time" just an excuse?

Sometimes it is not. Sometimes there are legitimate reasons to do something important later rather than sooner. There might be valid financial or career reasons for you and your partner to delay starting or expanding a family for a few years.

Still, you can do things *right now* to prepare for and move toward that future scenario, so that you continue to connect with the priority. These might include starting a savings account for your eventual child, joining a parent's forum, or volunteering with a children's charity. These actions do not have to be time-consuming. They are just enough to keep the priority live and top-of-mind. By not wholly ignoring or deferring your goal, you will indirectly work toward accomplishing it and feel more in control over the situation.

This indirect contribution benefits you on two levels. First, it moves you a little closer to achieving your goals. Some progress is better than no progress. Second, these small actions increase the likelihood that you will activate your priority down the road when the timing is indeed better.

3. MAKE PEACE WITH YOUR PRIORITIES

Some of the biggest drains on energy and soul are the internal mental battles in which we often engage. We give ourselves (and each other) a hard time because we set high expectations and standards.

Stop whining and beating yourself up. This accomplishes nothing.

Once you establish your priorities, make peace. Accept it and move on. When accepting a short-term trade-off, such as prioritizing A over B, ask whether B will ever become a future priority. If you no longer value B, drop it and focus wholeheartedly on A. If you expect B will become important in the future, then:

- Put a time limit on the B downgrade.
- Consider short-term actions you can take to connect to this future priority and to keep it "alive."

For example, a good friend of mine complains about not retiring early. He only half-jokingly says his kids prevent him from golfing full time. However, this is a choice he has made. He needs to make peace. He *chooses* to live in the most expensive city on the planet. He *wants* private education for his children. By focusing on the positives he can negate the downside of working several more years to pay the tuition bills. Moreover, there is a time limit (until his youngest child goes to college). He can do plenty right now to plan for golfing in retirement and connect to that goal.

Once you make the conscious decision to prioritize A over B, such as first-class education for your children over early retirement, make peace and move on.

ENRICH: KEY TAKEAWAYS: AVOID THE DEFAULT SETTING

We constantly confront choices large and small. "Life" aggregates thousands of discrete decisions. Some decisions we make consciously, others we make instinctually. Often, we do not make a decision at all; we just reflexively respond to someone else's agenda. That's how the default setting sets. To avoid the default setting, it's imperative to Narrow—to identify the core of the life you will build. Narrowing helps you direct focus and energy toward what's most important.

Charles Scott had the courage to reject the default setting. To do this requires awareness of what takes precedence. To achieve this, we have two valuable tools—the Mission Statement and the Hierarchy of Priorities. The Take Action exercises below will guide you to develop both. These two tools (plus other mechanisms we'll discuss in the next several chapters) will help you make choices and take actions that enrich your life. The goal is not to have it all—but to insist on all that matters.

- The default setting sets when we are unaware or ignore what's most important.
- The Mission Statement serves as your North Star.
- The Hierarchy of Priorities helps you determine what is relatively most important.
- When you Narrow, absolute priorities stand the test of time; zoom out to see the big picture.
- To avoid the default setting, take care of a personal priority first, do not delay the nonnegotiables, and make peace with your decisions.

We've now explored the first two steps in the ENRICH method. After you Essentialize and Narrow, the next step is to "Reach." This involves setting compelling goals and relentless Intentionality to get to where you want to go.

ENRICH: TAKE ACTION: CRAFT YOUR MISSION STATEMENT

The Mission Statement is your North Star—it helps frame focus and importance. Mission Statements comprise two parts: a vision and values.

Mission = Vision + Values

To create your Mission Statement:

1. Define your vision, where you intend to go. Take the long view. To articulate a vision, imagine the end and work backward to the present. These techniques might be helpful:

Amazon approach: Amazon uses a method called the Future Press Release to help define clear goals and strategies before a new initiative gets underway. This backward-working technique visualizes a press release *before* introducing the new product or service. This technique is powerful because it anticipates the new product's *success*—who benefits, the added value to the customer, and the decisions and processes leading to success. In short, at the start of the process, this approach nails The What, The Why, and The How.

Epitaph approach: Epitaphs are short, direct, and eternal. Consider the words to inscribe on your tombstone. How do you wish others to remember you? What is your contribution to the universe?

2. Identify your primary values. Values make effective Mission Statements and reflect who you are. The following prompts may help articulate your deepest values. Answer these questions quickly. Respect what first pops into your head; that is typically the most authentic response. Try to identify around three fundamental values, but no more than five.

    a. What one word best describes you?
    b. What life lessons do you most passionately want to impart to a young loved one?
    c. Who is important to you? What word describes him or her?
    d. Who do you most deeply respect? What specific quality or qualities do you admire in that person?
    e. If you had one rule to live by, what rule would that be?
    f. What is your legacy?

3. Merge your vision and deepest values into a single statement. Here is a real-life Mission Statement developed with the epitaph approach and other prompts in this exercise. (The professional

behind this Mission Statement is Alex Strah, whose case study and journey you will read about in chapter 13.)

"Be passionate about life experiences, commit to family and to deep friendships (people I can call at 3 a.m.) for life, and above all, never settle for average."

ENRICH: TAKE ACTION: BUILD YOUR HIERARCHY OF PRIORITIES

This exercise walks you through my process to identify and rank your cherished priorities. Alternatively, you can use the ABC method or Warren Buffett's approach, as I described earlier. Common priority categories include family, career, wealth, relationships/friendships, quality of life, enrichment/self-development, health, love, giving back, travel, culture, and education.

1. Focus on the end game. Think ultra-long term. Imagine your life in thirty or more years.

▸ Who are you with?
▸ Day-to-day, how do you spend your time?
▸ What does your lifestyle look like?
▸ How do you fund this lifestyle?
▸ What did you accomplish?
▸ What did you contribute?
▸ Is there any unfinished business?

Consider personal growth, professional growth, family, and community. Be detailed and specific.

2. Then ponder the most penetrating question: *What will you most regret not doing?* Contemplating future regrets is a sure-fire way to clarify your priorities.

3. Then focus on the next ten years, and ask yourself the same questions, especially: *what will you most regret not doing in the next ten years?*

4. Probe the Why. For everything that comes to mind, ask *why?* Then probe deeper, asking *why* again. Then *why* again? Hack at the branches to understand the root reason something holds importance.

5. Consider the most profound values you identified in the previous exercise ("Craft Your Mission Statement"). Do the priorities you identified reflect these values?

6. Finally, sort your priorities into four categories:

▸ Nonnegotiable Priorities
▸ Important Now Priorities
▸ Important Later Priorities
▸ Nice-to-Haves

This is your Hierarchy of Priorities. Ideally, you will have no more than three to five nonnegotiable priorities and no more than about fifteen priorities in total.

If you'd like a real-life example of what a Hierarchy of Priorities can look like, here's Alex Strah's Hierarchy, developed using the steps and prompts in this chapter.

NONNEGOTIABLE

▸ Enjoy a long life with my spouse
▸ Achieve financial security by age fifty-five
▸ Ensure my kids' happiness
▸ Maintain fitness and health
▸ Professionally, make sure work never feels like work

IMPORTANT NOW

▸ Be a parent my kids can talk to

IMPORTANT LATER

▸ Enjoy annual holidays with close friends
▸ Be a good and accessible friend
▸ Live in Europe for a year
▸ Offer trusted advice to startups, informally and formally
▸ Retire abroad by age sixty

NICE TO HAVE

▸ Learn something every day
▸ Travel for one-plus years with my spouse
▸ Attend significant sporting events—Super Bowl, Wimbledon, March Madness, World Series, NBA Championships, Olympics

REACH

What does it take to achieve a big-ass goal?

Should you aim for moonshots or incremental progress?

If life is a journey, where's the darned road map?

How can you double your chances of achieving your financial goals?

An enriched life does not happen accidentally. It requires effective goal-setting and relentless Intentionality to get to where you want to go.

ESSENTIALIZE **E** NARROW **N** REACH **R** IGNITE **I** CALIBRATE **C** HARNESS TIME **H**

We're now at the heart of the ENRICH method. In this third step, you will identify and target your most meaningful life, financial, and professional goals. To Reach, you will:

- Convert priorities into compelling goals (chapter 4)
- Create a Life Plan (chapter 5)
- Build Annual Financial Plans to support long-term financial objectives (chapter 8)

Because financial security underpins ENRICH, three chapters highlight financial security. Chapter 6 discusses the fallacy of The Number, the value of cash cows, and nine tenets for financial fitness. Chapter 7 explores how to reverse the economic paradigm and work your money. Chapter 8 puts these personal finance principles into practice by creating your plan for financial security.

Now, let's explore how to convert priorities into powerful goals and improve the probability of success. Buckle in. We cover a lot of ground in this step. Prepare to challenge conventional wisdom, and perhaps even your behaviors and beliefs.

CHAPTER 4

———

INTENDED OUTCOMES

"You've got to be very careful if you don't know where you are going, because you might not get there."

—Yogi Berra

"A good goal should scare you a little and excite you a lot."

—Joe Vitale

What does it take to get to Earth's extreme points?

For this chapter on goal setting and goal achievement, I spent quality time with two world-class achievers to understand their strategies and techniques. Adventurers, especially those at the top of their game, are an exceptional breed of uber-achievers. Nothing shouts big-ass goal more than breaking a world record—being the first, the fastest, or the sole individual on the planet to accomplish something.

THE EDGE, THE FOCUS

Adrian Hayes has conquered Everest, K2, and the North and South Poles. He crossed Greenland by snowkite and the Arabian Desert by camel. These feats are the culmination of a lifetime of goal setting. He set his first world record for reaching the three extreme points of the Earth—the North Pole, the South Pole, and Everest—in the shortest time (one year, 217 days). He set a second world record for the longest unsupported snowkiting journey in Arctic history, the 1,940-mile vertical crossing of the Greenland ice cap. No one had done this before, and no one has done it since. Hayes, a former British Army officer, also happens to be one of the world's few extreme adventurers with a corporate background. He currently advises the European Mars One project.

Hayes passionately and rigorously sets and *writes down* goals. Since age thirteen, he recalls detailing plans for escape and adventure. This planfulness did not originate from parents, nor from school; it came naturally. "The moral of the story," he tells me:

> When you write down goals, they come true. High achievers write down their goals. You can dream and leave your goals in the cloud. But when you make a concrete goal, then you have to achieve it. Goals are very different from To-Do tasks.

For Hayes, a potent goal has five qualities:

- Specific
- Measurable
- Time-bound
- Accountable
- Resonate with personal values

These first four criteria may be familiar. But resonance? Hayes explains that resonance is vital:

> Setting a goal has to align with my values, or it will fail. I always ask myself WHY I want to achieve it. I don't do an expedition to prove something to people. I do it for myself.

Obstacles can get between Hayes and his goals. Some of these are external, such as unpredictable weather. There are also massive inner impediments. Willingly enduring pain, hunger, exhaustion, and extreme discomfort in harsh circumstances for extended periods demands unimaginable levels of personal resolve. Which raises the question—when the going gets tough, how to persevere?

He attributes his persistence to several factors. He has ingrained tolerance and a legacy of British Army training to "grin and bear" debilitating conditions. Hayes also regularly reminds himself of the purpose of pursuing a particular goal—that's where the resonance comes in. Finally, the ultimate source of perseverance is the trust he shares with teammates, and that British sense of humor. Yes, Interpersonal Connectivity still matters, even when you're on a "savage mountain that tries to kill you," as *National Geographic* describes K2.

Hayes hyper-focuses on the big picture—his Mission and Purpose—and his goals cascade from there. His goal-setting process is as deliberate and structured as the goals themselves. He generally plans on a rolling two-year basis. Each year Hayes sets annual goals, usually five goals among three categories: professional, personal, and being. Hayes outlined his systematic goal-setting process.

REFLECTION

Mid-December: The process formally kicks off in mid-December, when he reviews the year that passed with colleagues and coaches. "There's a lot of energy at that time," he adds.

Winter Solstice: Hayes goes to an unusual place, such as Stonehenge, to reflect. (The winter solstice occurs when the North Pole tilts farthest away from the sun, the shortest day/longest night of the year.)

Last week of the year: The formal process shifts to another gear. Hayes spends 1:1 time with coaches to brainstorm and to put systems and processes in place. He identifies a theme for the upcoming year (for example, prioritization). He breaks down goals into one of the three categories: Professional, Personal, and Being. By December 30 or 31, the goals are set in stone.

The Being goal typically reflects a macro goal dedicated to that year's theme. This goal applies to the whole year and relates to self-improvement toward the person Hayes aspires "to be." The Professional and Personal goals are more tactical in nature, which he divides into quarters. A month is too short but a quarter is a natural equinox cycle, Hayes notes.

ACTION

Then he makes it happen, checking in every few weeks to ensure he stays on course. Once Hayes commits to a goal, he keeps the intent and its underlying motive in view. He writes goals down on paper, and that paper travels with him, so it remains readily visible. This helps him maintain focus.

REVIEW

At the end of March, Hayes conducts a small analysis. A much bigger goal review occurs at the end of June.

Given the extreme nature of Hayes's work, there are many variables beyond his control. He pegs his goal attainment success rate at around 75 percent, with most failures due to timing issues. Hayes pursues massive goals—climbing a mountain, writing a book. Sometimes delays occur, and sometimes goals need recalibration. And, sometimes, he comes to the realization that a "priority" is not actually a priority.

"The final thing is living in the present," he says to me as we finish our conversation. "We are told happiness comes in the present. Having the future gives us the edge, a focus. But future-oriented people have the danger of not being in the present. So there is a balance between living in the future and living in the present."

MOVE THE GOAL POST FORWARD

Annabelle Bond is the fastest woman and fourth-fastest person ever to climb the Seven Summits. She ascended the highest peak of each continent in less than a year and stands as the only record holder to tackle the Seven Summits beginning with Everest.

One of the harshest physical challenges anyone can pursue is to summit the world's highest peak. At 29,029 feet, Everest was just the opening act for Bond. She explains that although her pursuit of the Seven Summits was a spontaneous goal, she deliberately set out to become the fastest woman ever to accomplish this and to do so in under 365 days. "I went from goal to goal," she says. "All those goals stemmed from Everest."

Three hundred sixty days later, after overcoming a fear of heights and a tumor, she made history.

Goal setting is a religion to Bond. Goals appear in every aspect of her life, no matter how small, and keep her on track. Unlike Hayes, she does not limit the number of goals in view. She elaborates:

> In a day where there are so many distractions and deviations, it's crucial to have a vision toward what you're working on. For the Seven Summits, I lived and breathed Everest. There was not a day that went by that I did not think about climbing that mountain, even after getting diagnosed with a tumor.

Her upbringing nurtured this Intentionality. Her father, John Bond, greatly influenced her. Each year he mapped and shared his goals with the family. John Bond eventually ascended to Chairman of HSBC Holdings plc, one of the world's biggest banks.

Annabelle Bond's goal-setting strategy distills into three principles:

- ⑤ Visualization and focus
- ⑤ Preparation and planning
- ⑤ Competition and confidence

For *Visualization and Focus*, she describes this technique:

> I visualized Everest every day. I spoke about it nonstop. Just the mountain and its sheer presence dominated my thoughts. It was a positive picture of the mountain. I did not allow any negative thoughts to distract. Not a summit picture, not a post-summit picture. Just an intense visual of the mountain. I am going to do this. I am taking the opportunity and running with it. I wasn't into the glory; it was a personal journey.

Bond breaks down her vision into small, achievable goals, and *intensely focuses on the immediate goal in front of her.* Looking at Everest in its entirety, the route to the top is a series of intermediate goals: getting to Camp 1, then Camp 2, etc. She even subdivided Summit Day into four distinct sequential goals. She kept moving the goalpost until she finally stood atop Everest. Starting from the South Col on Summit Day, "I was only focused on the immediate next goal—not on the summit. The visual is, I need to get to the Balcony. Then I need to get to the South Summit, then the Hillary step, THEN the Summit."

In this goal setting, Bond advises, "You also have to allow for shit to go wrong. Sometimes goals need flexibility and reworking, but that does not have to affect the visualization. Be prepared to deviate." She cites her last day climbing Denali in Alaska. Eight hours into the summit climb, she encountered nasty weather. "I could have died if I continued," she says. "But I pulled back. The next day there were blue skies, and I made it."

Preparation and Planning: After establishing the goal, planning maximizes your ability to achieve it. Planning often makes THE difference in attaining a critical target.

Competition and Confidence: Bond continually looks for opportunities to build self-assurance. "You have to be prepared to take the risk, put it on the line," she tells me. "Don't focus on the what-ifs. So what? Look at the best in a situation, not the worst. You don't want the what-ifs."

This is the last thought Bond leaves me with:

> I think the majority of people who are successful in their endeavors, are not afraid of failure or have failed and learned

from the experience and moved along a different path to achieve their goals. Sometimes you need to believe in yourself enough to have the confidence to take a risk.

WHY PLAN AND SET GOALS?

In the previous chapter, we explored Narrowing to identify your priorities. In this chapter, you'll learn to transform priorities into powerful goals. These goals lay the groundwork for your Life Plan, which we will create in the following chapter.

What's the difference between priorities and goals? Priorities reflect relative importance, whereas goals reflect specific desired results—*intended outcomes*—that broadly support the priorities. A priority might be to become a parent; a goal might be to create a family by the age of thirty-five. Goals orient the mind toward a designed direction. The more your brain waves soak in intended outcomes, and the more you plan your goals, the higher your chances of accomplishment.

Planning and goal setting are such a vital part of the ENRICH method that it's worthwhile to take a moment to look at the qualities of powerful goals.

Some say there's research (sometimes attributed to Harvard, sometimes to Yale) that suggests that graduates who set goals earn ten times more than graduates who do not. That research never took place. Both mythical studies endure as urban legends because they reflect intuitive sense. It's logical that performance correlates with *setting goals* (especially writing them down) and *achieving* goals, as both of our world-class adventurers demonstrate. "A fool with a plan," the late financier, T. Boone Pickens, remarked, "can beat a genius without one."

This is evident everywhere. In a study of what Olympians do to prepare for competition, *Sports Psychologist* writes: "The best athletes had clear daily goals. They knew what they wanted to accomplish each day, each workout, each sequence, or interval."

Planning and setting goals deliver some fringe benefits, too. In *Flourish*, Martin Seligman notes that the future orientation associated with goal setting promotes a whole basket of intangible psychological benefits, including optimism and positivity. Seligman has demonstrated throughout his research the links between positivity and increased longevity, health, and life satisfaction. The bonus to setting goals: a longer life, in addition to improved focus and results.

A future orientation also expands your wallet. *The Wall Street Journal* reports that people who look forward ten years are dramatically better equipped financially than those with shorter-term horizons. *Entrepreneur* magazine cites having specific goals as one of six habits of millionaires.[3]

HOW TO CREATE COMPELLING GOALS

What makes a goal powerful?

AUTHENTICITY

A compelling goal speaks to your Mission and priorities. In fact, the goal is *how* you ensure your life reflects your priorities. The more the goal aligns with your Mission and Hierarchy of Priorities, the more it will motivate you, and the more committed you will be

---

3 Other common millionaire traits include waking up early, lifelong learning, taking time off, networking, and giving back. Do these sound familiar? These traits reflect the Essentials, and are characteristics of an enriched life.

to succeed. Consider: *Why do you do this? How are you (or the world) better off if you achieve this goal? What downsides will occur if you do not reach the goal? How does this goal support your nonnegotiable priorities?* All these questions probe authenticity.

To make a goal potent, add authenticity. Sometimes this expresses as "congruence" or "alignment;" Adrian Hayes calls it "resonance." Authenticity adds motive: why is this goal important to you?

SMARTA GOALS

Powerful goals should energize and inspire you to reach high. In the beginning of the chapter, Hayes shared his definition of a good goal. If you have ever worked in a corporate environment and set individual performance goals, most likely you have come across a SMART goal. SMART goals are good, but omit the concept of authenticity, which, as Hayes showed, plays a decisive role.

An enriched goal goes by the SMARTA acronym:

- Specific
- Measurable
- Accountable
- Realistic
- Timely
- Authentic

You will note this definition of a powerful goal is very close to Hayes's criteria, except we've added the notion of realism to arrive at this ENRICH definition. When you attempt to do something no one has done before, as Hayes does, realism doesn't apply. But for most people, an effective goal stretches your abilities but can still be reached with effort. Otherwise, the goal becomes a deterrent and is *ineffective*. Most people eventually give up when attempting an unreasonable goal. In other words, a powerful goal is neither impossible nor too easy.

SMARTA goals address the what, where, how, when, *and why* of an ambition. The more precise and focused a goal, the more effective it becomes. Define the intended outcome, not the activity, to achieve the result. How will you know when you complete the goal? By measuring it. This measurement could be a specific figure, or an event, such as reaching the top of Everest. A time frame is necessary for any SMARTA goal.

Consider a fitness example. "Exercise" is not a SMARTA goal. Thirteen percent body fat by July 1, on the other hand, is better. If you also identify the regimen that you will follow to reduce the body fat, and the purpose of getting fit, this goal becomes highly effective.

Alternatively, consider a financial example. "I want to get rich" is not a goal. It is a fantasy, which is aspiration without the hard work. A smarter, more effective goal might be to achieve $100,000 annual recurring passive income within ten years. Identifying the rationale for the goal—for example, to be able to spend more time with family—makes this goal potent.

HOW TO CONQUER ANY BIG GOAL

Our culture celebrates moonshots, those rare, radical breakthroughs. Google dedicates an entire division called X to moonshot R&D. Moonshots are sexy and crazy and inspire awe when they succeed.

However, incremental advancement drives most significant progress. Putting a man on the moon—the very definition of a moonshot!—is a case study in incrementalism.

The Apollo program was a series of incremental milestones NASA used to fulfill John F. Kennedy's audacious vision. Apollo 4 involved the first test flight of a Saturn V rocket. Apollo 8 marked the first crewed flight to the moon. Apollo 10 dress rehearsed the first lunar landing. Apollo 11, famously, resulted in that giant leap for mankind.

To formulate a compelling big-ass goal and propel yourself toward it, think big and act small. This is easy to remember as:

"visualize" then "incrementalize"

Visualize. In the enduring words of Leonardo da Vinci, "think well to the end, consider the end first." For Annabelle Bond, the image of the end was majestic Mount Everest. If your intended outcome is $100,000 in passive income, perhaps you picture several rental homes that could deliver it. Use whatever mental model you need to make your goals real and motivating.

However, for the process to work, go beyond imagining the pot of money at the end of the rainbow. An intended outcome visualizes both the *result* and the *obstacles* along the way. Visualization anticipates what lies ahead and recognizes barriers and challenges. The more detailed your vision of the *process* of achieving the goal, the more prepared you are to avoid or mitigate potential problems.

Visualization works for any intended outcome, from improving your golf game to attaining financial security. Just imagine, in specific detail, the action, the trajectory, and the result. *Forbes* reports that people who vividly describe or picture their goals are 20 percent to 40 percent more likely to accomplish them.

Incrementalize. When you visualize, think big. But act *small* as you work toward a goal. Reverse engineer. Work backward from your destination to determine appropriate milestones. This transforms a daunting goal into something manageable and achievable.

The milestones are actionable, intermediate, concrete steps that can be time-based or results-based. They connect the present with the future and propel you forward. As you advance from milestone to milestone, you move the goalpost forward. Progress is finishing ahead of where you started. Even small units of advancement can have a positive Impact on motivation levels and ultimate success.

Anabelle Bond's actions on Summit day reflect this incremental approach. Bond had been on Everest for *weeks*. Yet, even in the final stretch, she incrementalized. Bond deconstructed her final ascent into four intervals, each building upon the previous milestone, until she stood atop Mt. Everest.

AN ILLUSTRATION

Let's work through an example of incrementalizing a SMARTA goal. Since financial security is a chief characteristic of ENRICH, let's continue with the goal of engineering $100,000 in recurring passive income in ten years. To accomplish this, we need to get granular with everything that has to happen. What do you need to do now? If you start from zero, this process might involve dozens of in-between steps, each warranting a SMARTA approach. For example:

- Research and identify a target geographic location and strategy
- Network to identify a competent real estate agent and property manager
- Create a financial plan
- Secure a mortgage

- Acquire a rental property
- Lease the rental property
- Repeat

The Take Action exercise at the end of this chapter guides you to convert your priorities into compelling goals.

ENRICH: KEY TAKEAWAYS: INTENDED OUTCOMES

Adrian Hayes and Annabel Bond set world records exploring the extreme points of the Earth. To accomplish this, both developed systems to set and achieve their goals. The more you plan and set powerful goals, the higher the probability of success. In setting ambitious goals, visualize, then incrementalize. Stake your claim to the future, then reverse engineer and create intermediate milestones connecting your goal to the present.

- Planning and goal setting vastly improve your probability of success.
- Goals reflect intended outcomes and make your priorities come alive.
- Powerful goals share six SMARTA qualities, including authenticity and realism.
- To conquer an ambitious goal, visualize, then incrementalize.

After you convert your Mission and priorities into compelling goals, you need to get personal. In the next chapter, we'll discuss putting together a Life Plan, your personalized map to an enriched life.

ENRICH: TAKE ACTION: CONVERT PRIORITY TO COMPELLING GOAL

Think about a multi-month or multi-year nonnegotiable priority you identified in chapter 3. Identify something that will make life delicious, an outcome that materially enriches, perhaps one you regret not acting on sooner.

Now, convert that priority into a compelling goal:

1. Visualize the priority. Furnish your visual picture with vivid details. Consider the outcome and the obstacles you might encounter working toward it. Annabelle Bond's visualization technique described in this chapter may be useful.

   Incrementalize. With this visualization, work backward to establish milestones. Deconstruct the priority into achievable, actionable, intermediate steps, which can be time-based or results-based. Deconstruction converts a daunting goal into smaller, less intimidating and more manageable increments.

2. Identify the specific activities and results you need to attain that first milestone. Ask: What is the first milestone? How will you measure your progress and know when you achieve it? With effort, is the increment attainable? Is it relevant? Will it move the goalpost forward? When will you attain the goal?

3. Construct a detailed SMARTA plan that enables you to achieve that first milestone. Focus entirely on that immediate action. The subsequent markers are irrelevant if you fail to make it to the first one.

On Summit Day, Annabelle Bond only focused on the next immediate goal. The top would be out of reach if she did not get to the next goalpost.

A sports analogy illustrates why it's best to concentrate on the immediate next goal and not the ultimate prize. Bill Belichick ranks as one of the NFL's most successful coaches in its one hundred-year history. He has guided the New England Patriots to more Super Bowl appearances than any other coach has led their team to. Yet, each season, Belichick leads the team one game at a time. "We talk about today, and we talk about the next game," Belichick told CNBC. "And that's all we can really control. The rest of it will take care of itself."

4. Consider the potential obstacles you may encounter. How can you mitigate these obstacles? How will you respond to them? How can you prepare to overcome them?

5. Consider what you can do daily—starting today—to progress toward this goal. Be precise about what immediate actions you can take. Then act intentionally. Identify daily intended outcomes, and let them pull you along the path of progress.

6. Repeat. Once you hit the first milestone, repeat the process. Focus on the next increment.

7. If you have difficulty getting started or keeping yourself going, chapter 9 and its "Get Into Action" exercise can help.

CHAPTER 5

YOUR ASPIRATIONAL LIFE PLAN

"A goal without a plan is just a wish."

—ANTOINE DE SAINT-EXUPERY

"You may not be able to control the wind, but you can always adjust the sails to reach your destination."

—ZIG ZIGLAR

Life is a journey! How many times have we heard that? *A journey? What should I pack? What route should I take? For Pete's sake, where's the map?* These questions usually recede over time. We forget about the map and wing it through life.

I was in my late twenties when I realized I needed that map. Life was going great. I loved my job. I paid off my student loans and had just spent possibly the best three weeks *ever* with my family, during an epic sojourn in Africa.

And yet, heading home nine days into the new year, I felt directionless.

What next, I wondered? Where do I go now? What do I look forward to? Do I go back to more of the same? Or do I return with intention?

Sitting on the Dubai airport floor at 3 a.m., I sensed that if I was not fully awake and steering on this life journey, I might miss something important. Rummaging through my backpack, I found a crumpled piece of paper and a barely functional pen.

I had the tools to create a map.

I thought hard about my aspirations and jotted them down. I thought of the hopes that excited me, that pumped my heart and psyche. Scribbling down these thoughts, I felt alive, alert, and anxious to get on with the rest of my life. I felt enthused by this clarity of direction.

That initial plan captured about two dozen ten-year goals. I organized these highly specific goals into several categories and noted a couple of longer-term aspirations.

When I returned to the office, I reviewed and refined the goals, created a spreadsheet, and fifteen minutes later printed out the page.

Voila. I had a life map.

Those goals seeped into my brain. Bit by bit, my efforts became intentional and directed toward concrete, personally essential milestones. A few months later, on a quiet Sunday morning, I pulled out that spreadsheet and took stock. A few months after that, I took stock again.

After more than two decades of Life Planning, two things surprise me about this process.

First, I blew past those initial goals much faster than expected. I accomplished most of my intended outcomes within five years, and all but two within seven. (The aspirations to Be My Own Boss and to live at the beach took longer.)

As I put pen to paper in Dubai, I genuinely considered my ten-year aspirations to be highly ambitious stretch goals, possibly bordering on fantasy. They were substantial goals, to be sure. Creating a family, becoming a millionaire, and producing a television show were all on the list. I discovered that the mental process of articulating outcomes goes a long way toward actualizing them.

The second thing that surprises me is how much I enjoy the planning process and how embedded this process has become in my operating system. Life Planning energizes, excites, and incites, as you consider all the things you might accomplish over a period of time. It is an immersion in the "pleasure of possibility," in the words of cyclist-author, Jim Malusa.

A BUSINESS PLAN FOR LIFE
YOUR PERSONAL MAP

If you were to set sail from California to China, what is the first thing you would probably do, besides learning to sail?

Charting the course would be the first order of business.

Yet, in the journey of our lives, we often travel without charting a course and without a rudder. We drift. We accept the equivalent of floating in the seas, hostage to winds and currents. We cede control. We may end up somewhere we do not want to be. Perhaps we go nowhere.

It's not like planning *isn't* part of our lives. As individuals, we make weekend plans, wedding plans, educational plans, vacation plans, and career plans. Yet, ironically, we seldom develop a comprehensive personal blueprint for a vibrant and fulfilling life.

Every well-managed company develops business or strategic plans shaped by the firm's Mission, vision, immediate goals, and opportunities. Management reviews these plans at regular intervals to monitor performance and progress.

The Life Plan is analogous to a business plan. It's *your* map to an enriched life. The aspirations in this map should pull you with gravitational force in the direction you wish to go. This Life Plan builds upon everything we've covered so far: the Essentials, your Mission, Hierarchy of Priorities, and the bold goals that enrich your life.

Through SMARTA goals, the Life Plan conceptualizes the who, what, where, when, how, and why of your enriched life. (For a refresher on goal setting, you can refer to chapter 4.) This road map captures the things that move the needle of your life satisfaction, things that require a concentrated effort over time. Above all, the Life Plan should be aspirational and meaningful. It needs to inject a strong sense of "WOW!" and incite you to continuous progress.

The Life Plan also incorporates your strategy to create wealth, including short-term and long-term financial objectives. We discuss financial security in the next three chapters. We'll go over the top-line financial goals that you will develop and *plug directly into your Life Plan.* This is why the ENRICH method works; it connects your life *and* money ambitions.

This generic template shows you what a Life Plan can look like:

LIFE PLAN

Name:
Mission:
Date and Place Updated

	Current Year	Year +5	Year +10
THE BIG THING:	Big Goal #1	Big Goal #2	Big Goal #3
TOP PRIORITIES:	Goal #4	Goal #12	Goal #20
	Goal #5	Goal #13	Goal #21
	Why these goals are important	Why these goals are important	Why these goals are important
FINANCIAL:	Goal #6	Goal #14	Goal #22
	Goal #7	Goal #15	Goal #23
	Why these goals are important	Why these goals are important	Why these goals are important
PROFESSIONAL:	Goal #8	Goal #16	Goal #24
	Why this goal is important	Why this goal is important	Why this goal is important
FAMILY:	Goal #9	Goal #17	Goal #25
	Why this goal is important	Why this goal is important	Why this goal is important
QUALITY OF LIFE/ ENRICHMENT:	Goal #10	Goal #18	Goal #26
	Why this goal is important	Why this goal is important	Why this goal is important
HEALTH/FITNESS:	Goal #11	Goal #19	Goal #27
	Why this goal is important	Why this goal is important	Why this goal is important

To see a Real-Life Life Plan, you can refer to Appendix VII.

AN INVESTMENT THAT PAYS RICH DIVIDENDS

We will cover the step-by-step process of how to create your own Life Plan in the Take Action section. This may at first appear to be a complicated process, but it's not—if you know what you really want. That's why this plan is such a valuable tool. Synthesizing your aspirations on one page forces you to focus on what truly enriches your life. This focus is *invaluable.* There are four decisive reasons why creating a Life Plan works so well:

- It facilitates resource allocation: where to invest your time and money.
- It helps avoid time creep.
- It amalgamates and puts a time element on all your aspirations, so you can see how all your goals fit together (or don't). This

is the key benefit you don't get from just maintaining a list of goals.

- ❺ Plotting to the horizon increases your chances of getting there.

WHAT MAKES THE CUT?

When deciding what goals go into the Life Plan, you should consider two tests to determine what's important:

1. Ask: "Why?" Why do you want to do this? Why is this important? Drill down, repeatedly probing why this goal deserves your time and energy, and how it enriches your life. What are the benefits of action and the negative consequences of inaction? This gets to the authenticity of a goal, as we discussed in the last chapter.

2. Then ask: "In the future, will I regret **not** doing something?" Not having kids. Not getting an advanced degree. Not living in Italy for a year. If you will regret down the road not doing something, then you need to plan to do it. There is neither time nor space for regrets, which make you look backward. In formulating your plan, if there's any potential for disappointment—even if you are not entirely sure—include the things you'll regret not doing in your road map.

DETOURS

If you follow a map, what about detours? Detours, both expected and unexpected, are permitted and even encouraged in this process. The Life Plan simply keeps you oriented in the right direction. On many a road trip, the deviation can be the most interesting part. So, get off the interstate and take that country road. Just make sure that the detour will get you to your intended destination in a time frame you can accept.

THE LIFE PLANNING PROCESS

"Plans are useless, but planning is indispensable," pronounced Dwight D. Eisenhower. The benefits of Life Planning are in the process you establish to support this living and working document. Here are some general, overarching thoughts to keep in mind about creating a Life Plan.

Once you develop your Life Plan, create a process to review and update it. This will usually take the form of periodic performance reviews—several times every year when you will reflect on your progress. This reflection is necessary. Be sure to print a physical copy of the map and refer to it during the performance reviews. And always have one or two of the immediate goals visible in your daily life.

In chapter 4, we outlined Adrian Hayes's goal-setting process; it's an excellent guide to making an annual plan. Let's assume your Life Plan is based on the calendar year and runs from January to December. To formulate this yearly plan, start reflecting a few months before the new year begins. Below, I outline a time-tested planning method that covers a few cumulative hours over an October-January period. The process described here uses calendar years, but you can also use your birthday or some other date to mark the annual cycles.

- ⑨ Each October, reflect on what you want to accomplish in the coming year. Over the next few months, identify several big goals to focus on. Let these goals simmer and percolate to ensure their importance. Some goals will derive from other long-term objectives and move you incrementally toward a bigger goal. At least one of the annual goals should be fresh, opportunistic, and situational to whatever is happening in the world and your life at that time.

- In late December or early January, once the calendar resets and your mindset adjusts to the New Year, formalize these new goals. Update your Life Plan. Assess the goals individually and aggregately. Are they sufficiently ambitious and aspirational? Do they compel you? That's the WOW test. Also, make sure your goals are not too aggressive nor unrealistic. That is the sanity test. (We'll tackle this in a bit more detail in the Take Action section.)
- Lock the goals. You can either do this right away or wait. A delay might be useful. Financial objectives are central to this planning process. Closing the books on the prior year might not be possible until the December/annual financial statements are ready, usually in mid-January. Based on the previous year's results, revisit your economic goals to ensure that they are still appropriate: you may need to raise or lower your expectations.
- Once you lock the annual Life Plan, get on with life.
- Each April, July, and October, conduct ten-to-fifteen-minute performance reviews. Put these on the calendar. The October review starts the new planning cycle.

Planning only works when you stick to the process for the long haul. Develop a system that you can sustain. Life Planning works at the individual level, the couple level, and the family level.

Hold on! I am not a planner. How can I possibly do this? Planning is difficult when goals seem distant and abstract. So remove the abstraction. Think optically, explicitly, and vividly about your aspirations. Visualize the intended outcomes in detail, inserting yourself into the picture. In the image, include who you are with and the what, why, where, and how of what you do. Be super specific. Then visualize the intermediate steps to get from here to there. Then simply put those steps into words on paper. You can also shorten the horizons to make planning a more accessible process.

THE LIFE LIST

A companion tool to the Life Plan is the Life List, also known as a bucket list or a curiosity list. (The author, Paul Theroux, calls his the "Fuck It" list.) Here's where to put all your nice-to-have interests. The Life List tallies all the meaningful, but not high-priority, things that inject jolts of energy and fun. It can be an exotic and diverse index and is especially enjoyable to create socially over a few glasses of wine. Think out of the box. You can always edit later in sobriety.

You may want to organize your Life List in broad categories such as:

- Family
- Travel and Adventure
- Health, Fitness, and Sports
- Self Improvement
- Giving Back
- Fun Stuff

Some real-life Life List examples: Play eighteen holes at Augusta. Establish an orphanage. Attend the Oscars and Super Bowl. Finish a triathlon. Crash a black-tie wedding party. Dance all night in Rio.

A Life List provides inspiration, and you can expand the menu of possibilities as you come across new ideas that excite you. Try to tackle at least one item on your Life List per year.

The point is to keep adding, keep looking forward, and keep contemplating the pleasure of possibility. The Life List is a work-in-progress over a lifetime, which adds up to one helluva enriched life.

A TRANSFORMATION

By any objective standard, SuSan Tan at the top of her game. In cities across Asia, from Beijing to Bombay, this Singaporean has managed large-scale commercial projects for some of the world's biggest companies. A while back, she was also a card-carrying member of the Monday Morning Malaise club.

Several years ago I shared with Tan some core ENRICH financial concepts. She quickly internalized these ideas, starting a transformation that helped her move major goalposts and get out of a multi-year funk.

As I wrote this chapter, Tan came to mind. I thought she might provide a few sound bites for the book. I sent a cryptic text message suggesting we chat sometime soon. A few hours later, I received this marvelous message:

Absolutely!!

I resigned! My last day is on Tuesday, and I am on holiday to Turkey for two weeks. I start with my new company next month.

It all started with our chats at the Cafe in Dempsey to look into my finances. Then I bought my flat [apartment]. And worked for the promotion to a higher pay bracket. Then went into personal branding on Linkedin. Got a career coach. Confirmed my purpose and decided I needed more study, so I started my postgraduate diploma. It converts to a Masters next year. In the last year, I met with 50+ people and 20+ companies. Got five offers and accepted one.

This past year has been all goals and studies towards my

purpose of making a positive Impact on people's lives and organizations through workplace transformation.

So my timeline was: lost, lost, lost, lost, guided, coached, discovery, goal plotting, goal affirmation, action planning, goal detailing, action, action, action.

Tan exudes enrichment. Less than six months after receiving this message, I got another note from her. This one originated from Antarctica, where she'd just fulfilled another life goal.

Tan accomplished this turnaround in fewer than three years from our initial conversations about creating time wealth and igniting big goals. How? Planfulness and prioritizing financial security were the turning points for Tan. Once she articulated clear goalposts and how she had to change, she changed. A map made all the difference.

ENRICH: KEY TAKEAWAYS: YOUR LIFE PLAN

So far we've Essentialized and Narrowed. Now we're Reaching, inspired by the Life Plan. The following Take Action exercise walks you through each step of creating a Life Plan. I encourage you to spend some time on this exercise; it's worth it.

Just as her Life Plan benefitted SuSan Tan, your Life Plan plots the major intended inflection points of your life. It should inject a strong sense of "WOW" and synthesize your Mission and priories. The future-oriented Life Plan amalgamates everything we've discussed so far. The more you plan, the more you improve your chances of success. Otherwise, you may find yourself drifting and getting nowhere—or ending up somewhere you don't want to be. The plan itself is valuable, but the planning process is invaluable.

- The Life Plan serves as your personal map to an enriched life, blending your Mission, priorities, life goals, and financial targets.
- To determine which goals go into the Life Plan, understand The Why and don't leave any possibility for future regret.
- The ongoing planning *process* gives the Life Plan its potency.
- The Life List is a fun companion tool that tracks nice-to-have interests and aspirations.

Reach involves life goals *and* financial goals on your journey to create wealth in time, money, and meaning. How will you finance your enriched lifestyle? How will you ensure you achieve your ambitious financial objectives?

The next three chapters will show you how. We'll discuss financial security and how to create it. In chapter 8, you will develop an Annual Financial Plan. These financial targets *plug directly into your Life Plan.*

ENRICH: TAKE ACTION: CONSTRUCT YOUR LIFE PLAN

The Life Plan integrates your Mission, priorities, and goals to avoid "the drift" and help you to get to where you want to go. This plan should inject a strong sense of WOW and incite you to action. The Life Plan enables you to maintain focus and achieve your goals faster.

You can source a free soft copy of the Life Plan template at www. enrich101.com. Appendix VII provides a Real-Life Life Plan. To conceptualize *your* Life Plan:

1. Identify the annual cycle. Decide whether you will follow calendar years or fiscal years based on a significant date like your birthday.

2. Identify the time horizon. A ten-year horizon works well for many people. You can go longer or shorter, as appropriate—mark intermediate points. Depending upon the period, plot no more than three increments. For a ten-year horizon, marking one, five and ten-year points is appropriate.

3. Plan with the end in sight. Start with the intended outcomes at the end of your horizon and work backward. Use the goal-setting methods described in chapter 4 to plot intervals that support the realization of long-term goals. Incrementally build on your goals across the time horizon. Move the goalpost forward at each increment.

4. Focus on big goals that require a concentrated and sustained effort over time. More routine tasks, such as filing your taxes or getting a health check-up, belong on a To-Do list unless they require concentrated planning and effort.

5. Categorize the goals. Suggested Life Plan categories:

   a. *The Big Thing.* The Big Thing is an annual goal that makes a demonstrable difference to your quality of life and makes the year memorable. It could be a financial, career, family, or personal aim, which, when achieved, will materially enrich your well-being.

   b. *Financial goals.* Depending upon the economic priority, you may have several goals that support a long-term financial target. The Take Action exercise in chapter 8, Build Your Financial Security, guides you in plotting the financial objectives that this Life Plan section comprises.

   c. *Professional goals.* Focus on things you control, such as performance and professional development. Concentrate on areas that position and prepare you for professional success. If a promotion is the ultimate intended outcome, for example, what can you do to earn that? Double sales? Land a new client? Lead an internal task force? Become a thought leader by publishing an article or speaking at a conference? These are all actionable items over which you have control, and that you can chart in your Life Plan.

d. *Family/friends goals.* Highlight the memorable things you want to experience with the special people in your life. Milestone celebrations for significant events like birthdays, anniversaries, and achievements, belong in the Life Plan. Other special activities that require planning and concerted effort also make the cut. These might include a family reunion or an epic trip with friends. Essential goals for your kids, whether it's getting into the right pre-school or getting into college, also belong in the plan.

e. *Enrichment goals.* These improve the quality of your life and revolve around the Eight Essentials. Especially consider ways to increase social interactions and opportunities to nurture curiosity and inspiration.

f. *Health and fitness goals.* Invigoration is a fundamental part of an enriched life. Larger goals such as running a marathon or practicing a sport consistently merit a spotlight in the Life Plan.

6. Less is more. Try to target no more than ten goals across all categories in any given year. For a ten-year horizon with three milestones, try to have no more than thirty goals across all groupings. Even if you whittle down your goals to twenty over ten years, that's still a lot to tackle.

7. Prioritize your goals. There are two ways to go about this. One approach is to prioritize across the time horizon, and another is to prioritize for the current year. Whichever you select, do not identify more than five (and ideally, no more than three) high-priority goals.

Such goals should qualify as Nonnegotiable or Important Now in your Hierarchy of Priorities. *These are the priorities you firmly commit to achieving without fail.*

8. Apply the WOW test. Do these goals excite you? Inspire you? When you succeed, how will you feel? Will you enjoy a sense of achievement and progress?

9. Ask Why? What drives these goals? How do they enrich your life? List at least three positive consequences of realizing the critical objectives. What are the implications of inaction?

10. Check for sanity. Consider the goals individually and collectively. They should be ambitious but not impossible. In aggregate, is it physically, financially, and mentally feasible to work toward these goals, in all these categories, at the same time? Maybe not. You may need to parse the goals. Calculate goal feasibility. Make sure the goals are realistic and achievable with applied effort.

11. Ensure alignment. Include your Mission Statement at the top of the Life Plan. Check for congruence among the goals and your longer-term priorities.

12. Consider the impediments. Visualize the trajectory of your progress. What are the potential obstacles? How will you react? How will you overcome these obstacles, or at least mitigate their effects?

13. Organize. Create a Life Plan in a durable document you can review and update periodically. Excel works well because you can create tabs for each annual plan. Print your Life Plan. Make the plan or some of the goals visible in your daily life. Sticky notes on the bathroom mirror work well.

14. If a monthly to-do list is a tool that works for you, you can further deconstruct your annual or multi-year goals into smaller monthly increments. In this way, significant objectives cascade down into manageable, actionable tasks. A monthly to-do list is the right place to park routine activities like filing your taxes or going to the dentist.

15. Schedule quarterly performance reviews to maintain focus and track progress. Put these in your calendar. Activate calendar alerts.

16. Schedule the date you will begin next year's annual planning process. Put it in the calendar.

17. Create conditions to succeed. Implement some of the success factors from chapter 9 to increase the probability of goal attainment.

CHAPTER 6

FUTURE-PROOF YOUR FINANCIAL SECURITY

"The philosophy of the rich and the poor is this: the rich invest their money and spend what is left. The poor spend their money and invest what is left."

—JIM ROHN

"Too many people spend money they haven't earned, to buy things they don't want, to impress people they don't like."

—WILL ROGERS

Consider these extreme real-world situations:

A high-powered executive refuses to quit because his Number is $40 million. This executive wants to replicate his current multi-million dollar income forever. He does not enjoy his stressful job and works brutal hours. Severely overweight, he battles congenital heart disease. Yet, he plugs away until he gets closer to the Number. He cannot stop chasing that dangling carrot.

At the other end of the spectrum, Carla Jeffrey (a pseudonym) and her spouse are bona fide members of the professional elite with high-profile international business careers and Ivy League degrees. She recounts a dire situation:

> The moment that changed everything was indeed when my child was two weeks old—my first child. My husband came home. He had just quit his job because of a conflict of interest at work. I remember, literally, up at night, looking out the window, holding my baby, thinking, 'Oh shit, we don't have any savings. We don't have any Plan B.'

WHAT IS FINANCIAL SECURITY?

These two situations are extreme but not uncommon; they lurk everywhere, perhaps even among your friends. The high-powered executive can't walk away from The Number; it is his life's focus. Carla and her husband spent so little time thinking about money that they jeopardized their new family's stability when a career hit a speed bump.

Both situations reflect economic insecurity. If you want to enrich life, prioritize creating financial security. In chapter 5 you formulated your aspirational Life Plan, which synthesizes all your goals for an enriched life. Chances are many of those goals will require both *money* and *time* to accomplish. Financial security is the key to unlocking what you want.

What do I mean by financial security? If you have these five things, you're financially secure:

1. The ability to walk away from your job today.
2. Income independent from your primary occupation.
3. A comfortable cash cushion to cover twelve months of antici-

pated expenses, plus a provision for a significant unanticipated expense.

4. No manifestations of anxiety, such as loss of sleep, about money. Many issues might keep you up at night. Money should not be one of them.

5. Debt-freedom, unless the debt provides tax or financial benefits, such as tax-deductible mortgage debt. No consumer debt.

Financial security does not mean the sky is the limit on spending, nor does it mean curtailing spending and counting cappuccinos. It means funding a reasonable, comfortable, affordable lifestyle that enables you to realize your highest priorities. Financial security addresses both sides of the money equation—income and expenses.

Are you ready? Let's dive in.

THE RISKS OF *NOT* PRIORITIZING FINANCIAL SECURITY

Many professionals do not prioritize financial security when their careers are on the fast track. Many executives accept the sometimes-false security that a fat paycheck provides, without much thought to creating lasting wealth. The best time to create financial security is when you least need it. There are both offensive and defensive reasons why accelerating financial security should be every professional's urgent priority:

Offensive: Financial security gives you optionality at work and in life.

Defensive: Financial security lets you future-proof your finances. In the age of job insecurity, it reduces dependency upon a tenuous paycheck.

SHOCKS

If COVID-19 proves anything, it's the value of financial security. At light speed, this health pandemic induced an economic epidemic, disrupting financial markets. The pause in economic activity caused unemployment claims to surge faster than at anytime in history. During a crisis, there is enormous economic and emotional value to having financial security.

While the pandemic is the most vivid one in recent memory, economic shocks happen every decade or so. In the past twenty-five years, these shocks have included the 2008-9 Great Recession, the dot-com crash, 9/11, and the Asian financial crisis. We never know when an exogenous event might derail the economy.

The most financially secure strategy is to always be prepared. The stronger your financial position going into a crisis, the better equipped you are to weather the storm. If you have a sufficient cash cushion and emergency fund, and if your debt and cost structures are under control, you can take a long-term view. You do not have to make short-term financial decisions. Financial crises are great times to buy assets, but awful times to sell them. Panic selling destroys personal wealth and ravages financial security.

THE DISCONNECT

More than half of American workers expect to work past age sixty-five, according to the twentieth annual Transamerica retirement survey. That may be wishful thinking.

Even if you view the pandemic and other shocks as extraordinary one-off events, other persistent long-term forces jeopardize the security of a paycheck. Corporate consolidation, technological disruption, globalized competition, and outsourcing relentlessly chew up industries and spit out white-collar jobs by the thousands.

Unfortunately, most people start planning for retirement at age fifty. You should be ready to retire by then! ProPublica and the Urban Institute estimate workers fifty and older endure at least one involuntary job loss after age fifty. This 2018 headline from ProPublica says it all: "If You're Over 50, Chances Are the Decision to Leave a Job Won't be Yours."

You may not have as much time to prepare financially for the future as you think.

THE NUMBER FALLACY

So, how big is your Number?

That's a trick question.

I first encountered The Number at Columbia Business School, around graduation time. The Number, the pile of cash we hope to accumulate before—finally!—we can live the life we'd prefer all along, became a frequent Happy Hour topic. *Everyone* had a number. Sure, there was an element of chest beating in a boozy environment, but those conversations revealed a deep-rooted belief that The Number was THE end goal, a way to keep score in the game of "success." Many professionals associate The Number with financial security, and only *feel secure* when they attain The Number—*if ever*. They can't imagine an alternative.

Have you ever hiked a mountain and reached a crest? Just when you think you're arriving at the top, you discover a higher peak beyond. The Number is a perpetually elusive target. In a consumer culture that thrives on more and bigger, $1 million quickly multiplies as reference points evolve and enlarge. The treadmill does not stop. Asking "Who Actually Feels Satisfied about Money" in *Atlantic* magazine well before the coronavirus wrecked personal finances, Joe Pinsker wrote:

> These days, not even the rich feel rich. According to a recent survey by the financial-advisory firm Ameriprise Financial, only 13 percent of American millionaires classify themselves as wealthy. Even some of those surveyed who had more than $5 million across their bank accounts, investments, and retirement accounts said they didn't feel rich. If multimillionaires don't feel wealthy, who does?

The premise of The Number rests on a negative scarcity mindset. The conventional wisdom goes like this. Accumulate a finite resource—a pile of assets—then spend that pile, 4 percent every year, hoping it does not run out. The 4 percent rule has been the touchstone of retirement advice for more than twenty-five years.[4] The following comes straight from the Charles Schwab website retirement section:

> One frequently used rule of thumb for retirement spending is known as the 4 percent rule. It's relatively simple: You add up all of your investment and withdraw 4 percent of that total during your first year of retirement. In subsequent years, you adjust the dollar amount you withdraw to account for inflation. By following this formula, you should have a very high proba-

---

4   The 4 percent rule also undergirds the common myth that a net worth representing 25-x annual spending is required to retire. That's not true. When you work full time, you may have to live in a high-cost location. But if work becomes optional—which is the goal of financial security—you can elect to live in a high-quality but lower-cost locale. You may not need 25-x of your current annual spending.

bility of not outliving your money during a 30-year retirement according to the rule.

The 4 percent rule builds on historic actuarial tables. What if you live longer or retire earlier? Life expectancies are rapidly increasing. If you take care of yourself and champion the eight Essentials, living to one hundred is a reasonable target. Centenarians are the fastest-growing age group according to US census data. The number of people living to one hundred is expected to increase by 600 percent in the next several decades, because of advances in medicine and technology.

The Social Security Administration says one out of every three sixty-five-year-olds alive *today* will live past age ninety. Can your Number stretch that far?

Basing your long-term financial health on a depleting pile of assets is a risky strategy, especially when the time horizon stretches longer. This strategy leads to timing issues and anxiety about getting the timing or math wrong, resulting in all types of sub-optimal outcomes.

In other words, a financial strategy built upon The Number prolongs economic *in*security.

The United States has the world's widest retirement gap, according to the World Economic Forum. The retirement gap reflects the difference between what you have for retirement and what you should have. Several factors contribute to this gap: people live longer, the gig economy continues to expand, standard-of-living expectations continue to rise, and the US safety net has some holes.

The current paradigm to build wealth around The Number does not work for many professionals. By erroneously focusing on The Number, millions of Americans risk outliving their savings. A whole generation of retirees is unprepared for the future because their goal was to accumulate assets rather than to accumulate income to last a lifetime.

The SECURE Act, passed by Congress in 2019, recognizes this problem. This law is the most substantial revision to retirement account rules in decades. Among other changes, SECURE mandates that 401(k) accounts specify the asset's lifetime income potential. This income-based performance measure will help reorient metrics toward income rather than appreciation.

REVERSE THE FINANCIAL PARADIGM: CREATE CASH COWS

Thinking about financial security in terms of absolute net worth and The Number is how most people measure their financial health. And by extension, most people aspire to create wealth by chasing capital gains—by buying low and selling high.

But *you're* not most people. You're on a journey to enrich your life, and that necessitates a financial mindset shift. It's time to reverse the paradigm and *stop* working for your money and to *start* making your money work for you.

Your Resting Metabolic Rate is the rate at which your body burns energy when entirely at rest. This metabolism happens naturally, regardless of what you are doing. It even happens while you sleep. Your income should accrue the same way.

Ditch the Number. Instead, focus on lifetime income. Think cash flow instead of capital gains.

How do you do that? You turn your assets into productive, income-generating sources of cash you earn in your sleep. This is money you can count on coming in, month after month, creating financial security and optionality at work and in life.

These are known as cash cows, and they generate reliable passive income streams. These enriching income streams fulfill five criteria:

- ⑤ Passive
- ⑤ Recurring
- ⑤ Predictable
- ⑤ Tax-Efficient
- ⑤ Diversified

Common cash cows include rent, dividends, interest, annuities, royalties, and a business you own but do not manage day-to-day. Passive income differs from earned income, such as a salary or a side hustle, which requires your time. Passive income requires none of your time, and that makes it much sexier. Also, in the United States, some forms of passive income are taxed more favorably than earned income.[5]

When you engineer passive income through cash cows, you will thrive in an elite financial minority. Research from the 2019 Federal Reserve report on economic well-being indicates that 72 percent of American adults *do not have* any interest, dividend, or rental income.

To achieve real financial security, you need passive income sources that are predictable, recurring, reliable, and automatic. To reduce concentration risk you also need to diversify these income streams.

---

5   At the time of writing, the US tax rate for qualified dividends and long-term capital gains is 15 percent or 20 percent. Depending upon your income level, the marginal income tax rate on earned income can be as high as 37 percent.

That way, should one stream evaporate, the Impact won't be catastrophic.

There are three huge advantages to building wealth and financial security around cash cows.

1. *Longevity.* As long as you can live off the cash flow, you can afford to live forever. Longevity becomes a positive—something to strive for, rather than worry about.

2. *Holding power.* When you target The Number, you're counting on appreciation to generate value. With unproductive assets (i.e., those that do not generate reliable income), the focus rests on market value—which can go up or down. That yields anxiety, not security. If the value of an investment plummets, as many have during the coronavirus contagion, you might be tempted to panic sell. By prioritizing income, you get benefits from your assets other than their current valuations. You get cash flow, and as my former finance professor fondly preached, cash flow is king. Cash flow gives you more holding power and financial flexibility. It makes it easier for you to maintain a long-term focus even when asset values suffer.

3. *Legacy.* Financial security based on cash cows preserves the underlying assets. You can create generational wealth for your loved ones, or create an Impact on the cause(s) you care about through planned giving if that's important to you.

At this point, you may think, OK, I get the rationale for having cash cows when I eventually retire. But why do I need to create cash cows now, when I have a good job?

Beyond the Boy Scout rationale ("Be Prepared"), putting cash cows in place ASAP gives you the added benefits of financial *and* psychological compounding.

What is psychological compounding? Consider this: the distinction between theoretical and actual is vast. Theoretically having independent cash flows does not deliver the same feeling of financial security as actually banking the cash flows month after month. The longer the cash cows are in place, the more confident you become about their reliability, durability, and *the more secure you feel.*

Moreover, it takes time to turn unproductive assets into cash generative vehicles, especially if you pursue a real estate investment strategy. All the more reason to start early.

We'll explore the best way to create passive, diversified income in chapter 7. Before moving on to those strategies, however, we need to address a persistent and perplexing financial question.

HOW MUCH IS ENOUGH?

The short answer is: you probably need significantly less than you think, but the only way to know for sure is to do a bottom-up calculation.

In chapter 2, I presented some research indicating that the annual income sweet spot generally ranges from $75,000 to $115,000 for an individual and is around $200,000 for a family. Income satiation occurs at $200,000; anything beyond that is a bonus. If you remain unconvinced, consider three additional data points:

- David Clingingsmith, a Case Western Reserve University economist, examined the causal effect of family income on the frequency of negative emotions such as nervousness and hopelessness. He found that beyond $80,000, increases in family income have diminishing returns, with no marginal improvement in a person's negative emotions above $200,000.

- Purdue University research pegs the optimal amount of income for an individual at $95,000 for life evaluation and $60,000 to $75,000 for emotional well-being.
- Banktivity calculates that the average American needs $80,594 annually to feel financially secure.

Again, the point is qualitative and not quantitative. All these studies arrive at the same conclusion: we don't need as much as we might think. Consider spending during the COVID-19 lockdowns. Stores and businesses closed and consumer spending plunged; buying behaviors shifted from impulse to essential. Those weeks in lockdown demonstrated to many that, indeed, "less" can be "enough."

Once again, through the so-called 80 percent rule, the financial services firms propagate a misconception about how much is enough. Fidelity's standard advice, extracted from the retirement section of Fidelity.com, states:

> The 80 percent rule provides a guideline of what you can afford in retirement...If you know what your annual income is today, you can start the planning process by assuming you'll spend about 80 percent of the income you will be making before you retire every year in your retirement—that's known as your retirement income replacement ratio.

Eighty percent replacement income makes an intimidating threshold, especially for high-income earners. It creates the distorted perception that we need to work forever to fund retirement.

Drawing down 4 percent of savings or targeting 80 percent

replacement income are convenient rules-of-thumb. These rules-of-thumb might have worked in the past but their usefulness is questionable going forward, given elongated lifespans and challenging economic conditions. Collectively, these rules-of-thumb create the misleading mythology that retirement is more complicated, expensive, and distant than might be the case.

For many, significant expenses include saving for retirement, taxes, housing costs, and possibly educational costs. The only way to determine how much replacement income you need in retirement is to calculate bottom-up, recognizing that you will no longer need to account for savings and that you may qualify for some government retirement benefits, such as Social Security. If your income is tax-efficient, that lowers the hurdle as well. You might be pleasantly surprised to realize that your income threshold in retirement is much lower than you think—that is what I discovered. (We will do the math in chapter 8.)

This brings us to the final major theme in this chapter. Until now, our discussion about financial security has focused on *income*. There are two sides of the money equation. To get fiscally fit, we also need to address *expenses*.

FINANCIAL FITNESS—GETTING INTO SHAPE

When you got your last pay increase, where did that increase go? Do you consider yourself disciplined in spending and saving? Do you routinely and actively manage your personal finances and financial strategy? Are you on track with your monetary priorities?

Many think just getting a raise or a side hustle will improve their financial security, but managing outflows is just as crucial as increasing inflows. A reliable approach to financial fitness rests on nine tenets:

1. Know Your Numbers
2. Create a Cash Cushion
3. Save Before You Spend
4. Live Below Your Means
5. Eliminate Debt
6. Automate and Find Joy in Saving
7. Start Early
8. Always Think of TAKE HOME Income, Net after Taxes, and Other Expenses
9. Consider arbitrage.

1. KNOW YOUR NUMBERS

Thoroughly understand your current financial situation, your assets and liabilities, your income, and expenses. Get a macro picture of how you spend your money. Grasp your money movements to develop confidence in your finances. If you have a high income and do not know your numbers, chances are you will feel insecure. Conversely, if you have moderate income but understand your numbers, you may have much higher financial security than the high-income individual. (In chapter 8, we'll talk more about Big Picture Budgeting, a technique that can help you know your numbers without too much hassle.)

2. CREATE A CASH CUSHION

The situation Carla Jeffrey and her husband faced when they created a family *before* creating a financial safety net, is unfortunately common. The previously mentioned Federal Reserve survey reveals that about half of American households do not have emergency savings. Could you pay a sudden emergency expense? A feature of financial security is the ability to absorb unexpected bumps in the road. Build a cash cushion to help manage unplanned expenses. This emergency fund should ideally cover at least a full year's worth of anticipated living expenses, segregated but accessible in a liquid account. The cash cushion should also be able to provide for a significant unanticipated payment, such as a large medical bill.

3. SAVE BEFORE YOU SPEND

There are three ways to increase savings:

- Increase your income
- Increase your ROI
- Decrease your costs

Boosting income and ROI are somewhat beyond your control, so at first, concentrate on the area over which you have the most power: your spending.

The custom is to spend first, then save whatever remains. To reverse the paradigm, target your desired savings level (which supports long-term financial priorities) and fit your spending to whatever remains. In other words, the variable should be your consumption, not your savings.

Always be sure to pay yourself first. As we discussed in chapter 3, one guaranteed way to avoid the default setting is to first take care of your personal priorities. This same principle applies to engineering financial security. The battlefield-tested way to maintain the course toward your long-term financial objectives is to save first, then spend. Sequester your savings into an account separate from your day-to-day spending account.

In researching this book, I quizzed some professionals about saving strategies. Frequent and effective tactics include:

- Save one-third of your monthly salary. After making maximum contributions to retirement vehicles (e.g., IRA, 401(k)), segregate these monthly savings in another account. Another one-third of your monthly salary should cover all fixed and recurring costs, such as housing and auto. You can spend the remaining balance on a discretionary basis on things like groceries, dining, travel, and entertainment. "I find it important to have a separate savings account where I physically put aside the one-third I intend to save. This connects to a brokerage account, so I can do direct transfers fast. That way, it's easier to monitor how much I save, and it doesn't get mixed up with the spending funds," one professional explains.
- If substantial income comes through a bonus, "a good strategy is to save 100 percent of your bonus and adjust your lifestyle to your base salary," says another respondent.
- If your household has dual incomes, a great tactic is to live off one spouse's salary and dedicate the other spouse's salary to savings.

4. LIVE BELOW YOUR MEANS

If you spend less than you make, you will build wealth over time. As income rises, the temptation is to spend to your income level, not to your needs—that's called lifestyle creep. Be vigilant against it.

Focus on the big-ticket items that move your cost structure needle. Don't fret over the cappuccino vs. avocado toast. For many professionals, there are probably three significant hurdles to accelerating financial security: a house that's too large or expensive, a flashy car, and debt. For some, private education is another.

A big house—that glistening status symbol that embodies the American dream—may also delay your goal of financial Independence. Avoid social comparisons and stop trying to beat the Joneses. Move to a different place.

Maintaining a home is expensive. Research reveals that underspending on housing is the most significant factor in boosting savings. TD Ameritrade looked at the spending habits of "super savers"—those who save 20 percent or more of their income. Housing was the differentiating variable. Supersavers spend just 14 percent on housing, while the norm is 23 percent. When considering the price of housing, factor in all the running costs—the property taxes, the mortgage payments, plus lawn, security, furnishings, association fees, and other accouterments. Do you need so much house? Is it worth delaying your financial security?

A flashy car is another status symbol. If you cannot afford to pay cash for the car, you probably can't afford it. (Sometimes there may be financial advantages to leasing rather than buying an automobile. That is a different matter. The issue here is affordability and living comfortably below your means.)

5. ELIMINATE DEBT

If you cannot afford it, do not buy it.

Typical forms of consumer debt include mortgages, auto loans, credit card balances, and student debt. Excessive debt impedes financial security and undermines your ability to plan and prepare for retirement—and possibly to own a home.

If you have liability beyond a reasonable mortgage, prioritize debt reduction, starting with excessive credit card balances.

Only one-third of Americans pay off their credit card bills every month and do not carry a credit card balance. How insane! The average credit card interest is 15 percent and can go much higher. Use credit cards only as a convenience, not to buy something that you cannot afford. Do not be lured by points. Whenever possible, pay in cash. Physically handing over money serves as a psychological deterrent to frivolous spending, as opposed to paying with plastic.

6. AUTOMATE AND FIND JOY IN SAVING

The easiest way to ensure you habitually save before you spend is to automate your savings. Transfer savings from your paycheck into a dedicated account right after every pay period. Once you've automated, you will not miss the money, and your savings will be on autopilot. As you incrementally progress toward financial goals, saving will become an enjoyable and motivating activity. Making progress toward any goal satisfies, especially when the aim is financial security.

7. START EARLY

Modest savings can create significant wealth over time. Ken Jacquin, a venture capitalist and b-school classmate of mine, developed a long-term savings model (refer to Appendix III) that demonstrates three critical points:

- Compounding is powerful.
- That saving is a marathon and not a sprint.
- Starting early is a benefit.

8. ALWAYS THINK TAKE HOME INCOME, NET AFTER TAXES AND OTHER EXPENSES

Think net. Calculate what ends up in your pocket, free and clear. We often play mind games with numbers. We inflate our income by thinking in gross terms, meaning before taxes. Yet our spending comes from net income, after taxes.

Make financial decisions after accounting for taxes and expenses. To get the correct cost of anything, adjust to reflect after-tax dollars. That dramatically alters the price tag, especially for big-ticket items, and enables smarter financial decision-making.

There is an even bigger way in which we play mind games with numbers. Consider a high-paying job in an expensive coastal city. While the income might be high, so is the cost structure that goes with it. Calculate your net discretionary take-home pay, after all expenses, including housing, transportation, and taxes. A high-paying job in an expensive city may not be so lucrative after factoring the cost structure into the equation.

Always remember: It is not how much you make, but how much you keep, that counts.

9. CONSIDER ARBITRAGE

Arbitrage—taking advantage of price discrepancies—can lower your cost structure without compromising utility, enjoyment, or quality.

Geographic flexibility can help accelerate financial security.[6] To

---

6   You can time arbitrage as well. To do so, travel in the shoulder seasons, those periods just before or after the peak summer months, such as May and September. Time arbitrage is a way to improve the quality of the experience by sidestepping the busy, crowded peak months, and to save significant amounts of money on luxury travel.

engage in geographic arbitrage, consider moving to a high-quality, low-cost location, such as a low-tax or no-tax state.

Geographic arbitrage naturally occurs when professionals reposition for retirement. But why wait until then?

Explore geo arbitrage during your professional years. Social distancing measures have brought about a seismic change in the acceptability of remote working, which promises to reshape the nature of work. During the lockdowns, nearly half of US employees worked from home. The structural convergence of work and home is already underway, CNBC reports. Companies including Nationwide, Mondelez, Twitter, and Barclays are enshrining work-from-home arrangements. Mark Zuckerberg predicts that half of Facebook's workforce could work remotely within ten years.

When considering geographic arbitrage, think global. With a flattened labor market that lets companies source stay-at-home workers anywhere, why should you limit your options to your home country? There are usually some very enticing tax advantages, career advantages, and cultural advantages to working and living abroad. For Americans, the United States Government taxes citizens on worldwide income. However, there are tax provisions that enable expatriates to reduce federal tax liability on earned income by over $200,000.[7]

Having lived outside my home country for more than half my

---

7   Federal taxation excludes the first $105,900 in foreign earned income. The rules for state taxes vary by state; many states also offer an exclusion. Similarly, qualified housing expenses up to $103,900 are deductible from taxable income. Of course, you will be responsible for host country taxes. Most countries have tax treaties to avoid double taxation. Unless you relocate to a jurisdiction with higher marginal taxes than the United States (say, Sweden or France), your tax liabilities should be lower as an expatriate.

life, I attest to the culturally enriching merits of living abroad, in addition to the financial perks.

ENRICH: KEY TAKEAWAYS: FINANCIAL SECURITY IN THE AGE OF JOB INSECURITY

There are both offensive and defensive reasons to accelerate financial security. Offensively, financial security creates optionality at work, so you can dedicate your time to what matters most—the essence of an enriched life. Defensively, future-proofing your finances helps absorb economic shocks and insulates from long-term downward pressures on professional compensation.

Financial security addresses the income *and* expense sides of the money equation. When you engineer cash cows (income) and get financially fit (expenses), you will place yourself on a stable trajectory toward financial security.

- Financial security offers several benefits, including the ability to walk away from your job today.
- To create financial security, forget The Number: think cash flow instead of capital gains.
- ENRICH cash flows are passive, recurring, predictable, tax-efficient, and diversified.
- We don't need as much as we think, but the only way to know for sure is to do the math.
- To get into monetary shape, follow the nine tenets of financial fitness.

Turn the page to explore some strategies to create cash cows and work your money.

CHAPTER 7

WORK YOUR MONEY

"If you don't find a way to make money while you sleep, you will work until you die."

—Warren Buffett

"For tomorrow belongs to the people who prepare for it today."

—African proverb

Reversing the financial paradigm requires you to *work your money.* That means taking control and turning your finances into productive assets. Most likely, this also involves a shift from chasing capital gains to creating cash cows—passive, predictable, recurring income streams.

MY EXPENSIVE FINANCIAL AWAKENING

A decade ago, when I tried to create wealth through capital gains by buying low and selling high, I lost some spectacular amounts of money. Some of these losses were due to timing. Market sentiment easily influenced me, and I routinely bought high and sold low. Some of these losses resulted from trying to outsmart the market, as I pursued the latest investing fads my banker friends talked about over drinks. Some of these losses were due to "investing" in costly, complex notes structured on derivatives. It was the Wall Street equivalent of going to Vegas and betting on black. I never won any of those bets.

After one such excruciating loss, I had a heated discussion with my financial advisor, a quintessential Swiss private banker whom I originally hired years earlier because I was *too busy* to think about investments. It was a testy conversation; I was finished with expensive banker advice. In a rare moment of honesty—the kind that makes a Hollywood script—this banker, under fire, unintentionally revealed the financial services industry's dirty little secret. "You will never create real wealth this way," he told me. "Our job is to make sure you gain a little and don't lose a lot. If you want to create wealth, there are three ways to do it: Your job. Real estate. Or private equity. That's how you create wealth."

I fired him not long after that conversation, not because of his honesty, which I appreciated, but because I realized his irrelevance, and perhaps even detriment, to my financial security.

Many people believe relying on an asset manager and chasing capital gains in the stock market is the way to create wealth. For a long time, I thought so too. But relying on someone else and counting on appreciating assets—even if you get the timing right—may not provide the financial security you seek.[8] Emotionality easily takes over when the market melts or skyrockets. For example,

---

8   Some people do well buying low and selling high. My partner, for example, trades stocks every day and makes good money by applying technical analysis. But while he has a track record in generating capital gains, this source of income is neither passive nor is it dependable. Also, this principle of investing for income vs. hoping for capital gains serves as an effective filter. While editing this chapter, I reviewed a tempting investment in a real estate opportunistic fund offered by a major fintech platform. There were many compelling aspects of this investment—except the over-reliance on appreciation. Asset prices may not increase in the fund's time frame. I passed on this investment.

during the coronavirus market dislocations, even acclaimed buy-and-hold investor, Warren Buffett, uncharacteristically dumped entire positions in four airline stocks at a steep discount. Playing the stock market does not produce dependable, predictable, reliable wealth. It is situational, and market movements are way beyond your control.

Through a painful and expensive decade of foolish investing, I learned you cannot outsource creating financial security. *You* have to take control of your financial future, make time, make a plan, and own it. You have to get into the driver's seat. You can outsource the implementation of the game plan, but the plan itself needs to be yours.

Among savers, the number of professionals too busy to make their money work startles me. "I don't have time" is a common refrain. Ironically, some of those who say it, work in the financial services industry. I met one such person, Hannah, at a dinner party. She is a high-flying banker for a major European firm. If anyone appreciates the power of compounding, it should be a banker. Yet Hannah's savings sit idle in a standard bank savings account, which generates no yield. Hannah forfeits the wealth-boosting power of compounding.

Hannah does not work her money, and as a result, will work for it for a long time.

MY JOURNEY TO FINANCIAL SECURITY

There are many trajectories to financial freedom. The best strategy you can own, sustain, and ultimately use to achieve your goals. You need to create dependable, recurring income while you sleep. Make sure the route you take leads to your intended destination in an acceptable time frame, and that each month you incrementally progress toward your ultimate financial goal.

Here's my story.

My path toward financial security began with that first Life Plan, which I drafted in the mid-'90s. In that plan, I aspired to Be My Own Boss before I was fifty. By that age, I did not want to work for anyone but myself.

Around that time, I made my first real estate foray. It flopped big time. Upon the advice of a family member, I bought a single-family home in an "up and coming" neighborhood, sight unseen. I planned to turn this house into a rental property. I soon realized nobody wanted to live in the area, much less rent a house there. There were few people and fewer jobs in that location. Had I visited the property before I purchased it, I would have immediately recognized the opportunity fallacy. However, I was lazy and did not make the time to do my homework. I did not "own" the strategy.

Over the next decade, that real estate misfire led to the Swiss banker relationship. Meanwhile, despite my investing folly, I continued to save more money than I spent. Financially, I still came out ahead each year. Yet, that self-imposed deadline to Be My Own Boss was creeping closer, year by year. Although I saved money from my corporate paycheck, my assets were not productive; they did not reliably generate cash. The wake-up call was my departure from the Hollywood studio. I was asset-rich, so to speak, but cash flow poor. I realized the importance of cash flow and the need for a very different strategy if I was going to Be My Own Boss by the age of fifty.

I Ignited a self-directed plan to accelerate financial security by venturing back into the largest asset class in the world—the American single-family home. This time, I invested the time, did the homework, and relied upon experienced professionals to help me implement the plan. I repositioned assets and poured savings into real estate, acquiring rental properties on an annual basis during family vacations to California. Some tourists go to the Golden State to visit Disneyland and buy Mickey Mouse hats. The Millers house-hunted and bought investment homes as souvenirs. We worked hard, sometimes surveying dozens of properties in a week and maneuvering through a competitive market. Yet, those were fun family trips.

Within five years of making time and taking ownership of my financial destiny, I achieved the freedom to Be My Own Boss before my fiftieth birthday.

As I incrementally gained experience and confidence in real estate investing, my strategies evolved to maximize take-home income and minimize time hassle.

My real estate portfolio concentrates on specific locations in California and Kentucky and focuses on solid middle-class single-family homes. These are quality homes for reliable tenants. California offers good appreciation potential if you acquire a property at the right price, but the cash-on-cash yield is less attractive. Kentucky offers attractive cash-on-cash returns, but capital appreciation is more modest. Both markets have long histories of population and job growth, plus stable rental demand.

By concentrating on properties in two locations, over time I developed some geographic expertise and modest economies of scale with a support system of trusted property managers, realtors, and insurance, tax, and legal specialists. This support system reduces the demands on my time. I built this US property portfolio while living in Hong Kong and running a dynamic company as a full-time job. If I can engineer real estate cash cows by remote control from the other side of the world, anyone can.

It hasn't all been peachy. As a property owner, I experience the gamut of headaches. In California, I changed property managers multiple times until I settled on a capable management firm. Before then, I encountered some difficult tenants. (I've found that the more established the property management firm, the more reliable the tenants.) Annoying home associations, and leaky roofs, showers, and toilets are some of the other issues that accompany land lording.

Fortunately, I do not receive phone calls about those issues. I outsource day-to-day operations to established management companies. This support team is the key to passivity. My role is to manage the managers; this typically requires less than an hour each week. My work mostly involves making decisions, such as approving expenses above pre-agreed thresholds or authorizing rental agreement terms. The managers handle all incoming and outgoing monetary flows and accounting, and all tenant relationships. Each month like clockwork I receive financial statements and deposits into my bank account. These houses are cash cows and fit the ENRICH criteria: passive, recurring, predictable, automatic, and tax-efficient.

WHY REAL ESTATE ENRICHES

In the not-too-distant past, structuring passive income was simpler. Investors with decent nest eggs could invest in bonds, CDs, and fixed deposits, and these instruments generated enough interest to live comfortably. However, today's ultra-low (or *negative*, in some countries) interest rate environment makes this especially challenging. Central banks around the world are in no position to raise interest rates anytime soon…if ever!

When hunting for cash cows, there are many asset classes to consider—including dividend and preferred stocks and high-grade corporate bonds. Among all asset classes, however, real estate best supports the ENRICH philosophy and offers attractive tax benefits. Other investors agree. Investor purchases of US homes reached all-time highs in 2019.

Depending on where you are on the investment spectrum (whether you're just getting started or are an experienced investor), investing in real estate may be actionable or aspirational. Either way, consider its merits. Do not dismiss real estate because you perceive it to be beyond your means. Please hear me out and read on, then decide for yourself.

Real estate best supports the ENRICH strategy for financial security because it offers:

- Tangible, real assets
- Rising rental demand (national median rent hit an all-time high in 2019, according to *The Wall Street Journal*)
- Inflation-protected cash flow (rental rates generally increase with inflation)
- Encourages long-term focus because of the friction in buying and selling
- Significant tax advantages (remember, what counts is how much you keep)

Throughout this book, we have discussed the value of creating control and optionality. You get that with direct real estate investments. If you directly buy a real estate asset, YOU decide whether and how to upgrade, rent, or sell the property, and for how much. You're in the driver's seat. When you invest in public markets (e.g., buying stocks) you're only along for the ride.

The goal of ENRICH is to help you create wealth. Real estate affords you the ability to create wealth *exponentially*. If you finance a real estate purchase, your tenants will pay off your debt. If you do not finance, rental revenue streams can fund future acquisitions. There's more: American inheritance laws favoring real estate allow you to create *generational* wealth as well.

Although our primary objective is to structure cash cows, real estate also happens to be one of the best asset classes for long-term capital appreciation. The property market is cyclical and seasonal, and real estate is inherently local. Different markets behave differently. As in all asset classes, prices go down as well as up. Historically, however, real estate has been a dependable store of long-term wealth. Although the housing market catalyzed the 2008-9 recession, the US housing market has withstood all other recessions since 1980. Even during the 2008-9 recession, rental prices rose for three-bedroom properties as housing prices fell. (At the time of writing, it is too early to gauge the Impact of the coronavirus recession on long-term property values.)

In the Appendices, we will go deeper into the practicalities of creating cash cows. Appendix IV surveys common cash generative asset classes. Appendix V details why among these asset classes, real estate most enriches, and explains the favorable tax treatment for American investors. Appendix VI outlines four issues—where, what, how, and how much debt—you'll navigate to create real estate cash cows and highlights some common real estate investment strategies. The locations that make for good real estate investments may surprise you, and real estate investing is probably more accessible than you may think. Appendix VI also outlines some proven strategies for beginner real estate investors and introduces some fintech platforms that make the process easy.

ANOTHER PATH TO FINANCIAL SECURITY

To see an approach different from mine, here's how Singaporean, Hui Keng Ang ("HK" for short) worked his money and accelerated financial security.

The Job no longer inspired Ang after a change in bosses. He realized the urgency of financial security and accelerated a three-year plan toward debt-free living, which included paying off his mortgage. He achieved this ambitious goal in just over two years. Initially, the end goal was not to retire; it was to create optionality at work.

Financially secure a couple of years later, Ang took a year off to chill and travel, after more than two decades in finance and general management roles with a multinational. He expected to return to the corporate world after the sabbatical.

Then something curious occurred.

Ang observed mobility limitations among older travelers. That motivated him not to sacrifice to old age the benefits of relative youth and an active lifestyle.

"My whole perspective on life, money, investments, and work had shifted," Ang recounts. He discovered two things during that sabbatical: he did not want to go back to work, and he did not have to. "Retirement and savings are just a function of lifestyle," explains Ang.

At the end of the sabbatical, Ang assessed his options. An accountant by trade, he scrutinized his track-record investing with a trusted international bank. He calculated that the bank made more money *from* him than *for* him. That was the wake-up call to take control. "When we buy a new $1,000 gadget, like a phone," he explains, "we research the options, compare prices, and do homework. We blindly turn much more money over to an investment or relationship manager. We don't even think about it or ask any questions!"

Ang realized the unfair relationship with financial services firms: the banks and brokerage houses always make money on your account. They make money when you buy positions, and they make money when you sell. The banks have no skin in the game. You carry all the risk and bear all the potential loss.

In taking control, Ang cut out the intermediary. Today, he actively manages the assets he accumulated during his years as a corporate warrior. "All my years of accountancy didn't prepare me at all for investing and for making my money work harder," he says.

When I interviewed Ang for this book, he had recently returned from a European trip. Back home in Singapore, he spends his days investing, studying technical analysis, and enjoying life.

He has two investment buckets. He invests 75 percent or more of his assets for long-term performance. This portfolio mechanically generates monthly and quarterly dividends. Because Ang has a long-term perspective, he anticipates this portfolio will also appreciate over time, giving him a capital gains bonus. "I don't wake up in the morning and worry about these investments," he tells me. "I look at the portfolio once a quarter." Tactically, this long-term portfolio spans the US, Hong Kong, and Singapore capital markets in a combination of Electronic Traded Funds (ETFs), futures, and bonds. Ang does not invest in property because of the capital requirements.

He opportunistically invests roughly a quarter of his assets for capital gains, trading short-term positions, sometimes within a day, at most within a few weeks. He views this investment bucket as risk capital, which does not affect his financial security and ability to provide for his family.

"I'm very clear on my monthly financial commitments," Ang says. He does not risk future expenses through this trading, and separately funds his three college-age children's education.

He concludes, "Investing doesn't mean you don't work so much. I work hard. I enjoy what I do. I enjoy the feeling of satisfaction and achievement. Instead of working for money, money works for me."

MY STORY, CONTINUED

Earlier I described my expensive financial awakening and the long journey toward financial Independence. There is more to the story, folks. This is where it gets interesting.

After spending a quarter century methodically planning how to Be My Own Boss, I hit two major speed bumps early into my retirement. Twelve hours after permanently leaving the workforce, I learned that a private equity real estate investment had decided to cash out. This torpedoed my financial plan, leaving a noticeable hole in my anticipated cash flow. A once reliable source of tax-efficient passive income would soon disappear. I had to scramble to redeploy the proceeds into productive assets.

Then COVID-19 infected everything.

The first moral of the story: shit happens. Your financial portfolio needs to have shock absorbers—a sufficient margin (10 percent at a minimum, 20 percent-plus ideally) to cushion the surprises that inevitably line the path to financial security. Do not let a pothole turn into a sinkhole. Durability, flexibility, and diversification are essential to robust, reliable, and long-lasting financial security.

The second moral of the story: stress test your plan. Make sure your assumptions are realistic and do not rely on perfection. Consider multiple downside scenarios. If you can endure the downside scenario, however unlikely, then you have engineered bona fide financial security. Stress testing also involves understanding your risk tolerance.

AN OPPORTUNITY?

In the aftermath of the sharp and abrupt decline in economic activity during the COVID-19 pandemic, there are natural questions about whether it's still possible to engineer financial security, and how real estate cash flows hold up.

Now, it's not only possible but urgent that you work your money. When you're buying, selling, and counting on appreciation, bull and bear markets matter. However, emphasizing cash flows reduce sensitivity to market sentiment. If anything, a bear market is an opportunity to accelerate financial security—to acquire quality cash generative assets on sale. The 2008-9 financial crisis presented a historic investment opportunity, and the coronavirus recession may do the same. With real estate, some previously overpriced markets might become attractive. In addition, ultra-low mortgage rates support housing valuations.

This coronavirus shock did affect some real estate cash flows. Immediately hit commercial sectors include retail and offices; commercial retail/office tenants wasted no time to renegotiate leases. The immediate Impact on apartment rental collections was smaller than might have been expected. The National Multifamily Housing Council Rent Payment Tracker reports 93 percent of apartment households paid rent fully or partially in May 2020—versus 95 percent for the same period in 2019. This survey aggregates data from more than eleven million professionally managed apartment units in the US.

It is still too early to assess the long-term Impact of the pandemic on the property market. While capital markets react instantaneously, adjustments in real estate valuations take time.

CAVEATS

Own your strategy for financial security. This may or may not also involve money managers. For some investors, professional management can play a supporting role. If you use a financial advisor, only pay for advice through a flat fee or a management fee based on the percentage of assets under management. Never compensate a financial advisor through commission. Make sure your interests align with your advisor's and keep fees low; they drag performance. In today's flat yield environment, every basis point matters, especially with stock and bond funds. However, do not be penny-wise and pound-foolish. A highly competent asset manager may merit a premium.

Understand the tax implications and fee structures of your investment decisions fully. Taxes can change an investment's attractiveness. After factoring in taxes and fees, an investment might be much less pretty, or perhaps surprisingly beautiful.

Diversify, diversify, then diversify some more to reduce concentration risk.

Always remember the law of gravity: asset prices go up, and asset prices go down. You're in it for the long haul.

Finally, this book's strategies and tactics derive from personal experience and should not be considered professional financial advice. Always assess your own personal and financial situation and consider consulting a financial professional before taking any financial action, including the strategies discussed in this book.

ENRICH: KEY TAKEAWAYS: WORK YOUR MONEY

To work your money, take control and create productive assets. Counting on asset appreciation and chasing capital gains is neither predictable nor recurring—it is situational, and markets go up and down, sometimes irrationally. For real financial security, think cash flows instead of capital gains.

This chapter explores alternate paths to financial security. Although our paths differ, HK Ang's approach to financial freedom and my own share core ENRICH principles. Both involve taking control and making a plan for accelerated financial Independence. Both involve a high degree of passive cash flow and a long-term view (in Ang's case, with 75 percent of his portfolio). Financial fitness—knowing your numbers, saving before spending, and eliminating debt, all covered in chapter 6—underpin both approaches. Ang's path and mine both led to optionality at work and freedom to spend time wealth on what matters most.

Whatever road you choose, get in the driver's seat. To work your money:

- Take control and turn your finances into productive assets.
- Make time, make a plan and own it.
- Real estate best supports ENRICH cash cows because of predictable, recurring, tax-efficient and inflation-protected income, plus the capacity for exponential and generational wealth creation.
- Build shock absorbers to guarantee real financial security.

The next chapter will teach you how to work your money *practically* by building your financial plan. This marshals all the principles we've discussed around financial security, goal setting, and goal achievement.

CHAPTER 8

BUILD *YOUR* FINANCIAL SECURITY

"The best way to predict the future is to create it."

—Peter Drucker

"Most people don't plan to fail, they fail to plan."

—John L. Beckley

Let's quickly recap our progress together. In chapter 5, we discussed the merits of a Life Plan, your personal road map to an enriched life. This Life Plan captures everything that enriches your life, including short-term and long-term financial objectives. In chapter 6, we explored why it's important to accelerate financial security and how to get financially fit. In chapter 7, we considered two different ways to build cash cows and financial freedom.

Now we get practical. Let's implement what we've learned. In this chapter, you will discover how to build Annual Financial Plans to work your money. The financial goals you develop *plug directly into your Life Plan*, thereby unifying your life aspirations with your economic ones.

This warrants a couple of questions. What are your financial goals? How can you achieve them?

DOUBLE THE LIKELIHOOD TO HIT YOUR FINANCIAL GOALS

Achieving financial security will likely involve concerted efforts on both the income and expense sides of the equation over several years. Your Annual Financial Plan (AFP) is an operating plan that bridges the present to your long-term financial targets. Put another way, think of your Annual Financial Plan as a yearly budget with a long-term view. It details the steps you will take to hit current financial targets and remain on-track toward your long-term financial goals.

I can already hear some grumbles. What? This guy wants me to create another plan? I don't have time for this! And it's not necessary.

That is what I used to think. I did not create a personal/household budget until my early forties. I had neither spending nor saving issues. I had a good paycheck and a good job, and I was able to tuck away some money at the end of each year. *Why budget?* I thought. *I have better things to do.*

I was utterly wrong.

My experience is not unique. Many executives who "do well" professionally often do not have a rigorous, or for that matter any, financial plan.

Creating an annual budget to understand your numbers is the one thing you can do *right now* to increase the probability of achieving financial security, regardless of present economic circumstances.

The awareness that comes from systematic budgeting helps you focus on issues that move the financial needle. Ultimately, financial security is emotional. It entails building *confidence* and *feeling* secure.

Once I started budgeting regularly, I felt more financially grounded because I finally *understood* my money flows. Before long, I began to enjoy the process outlined in this chapter. Now I cannot imagine *not* investing the time for these simple planning and monitoring functions.

Financial security does not often happen accidentally; building and sustaining it requires focus and effort. Even fortunate people who benefit from a substantial windfall need a plan to maintain their newfound wealth. Take lottery winners. *Fortune* reported that almost one-third of them eventually declare bankruptcy.

Developing Annual Financial Plans makes it much more likely that you will hit your goals. *Money* magazine says that people with written financial goals are *twice as likely* to honor monthly savings goals. According to research by Charles Schwab and Wells Fargo/ Gallup, people with written financial goals are also almost *twice as likely* to feel they have sufficient resources to maintain their lifestyle when they retire.

There is zero downside to creating a financial plan and a whole lot of upside. Approach this planning with the mindset that you are creating a business, which you are—the business of a financially free YOU!

AN AZTEC MODEL

In chapter 4, we examined how to create compelling goals: visualize, then incrementalize. This goal-setting process especially holds true when it comes to building financial security, which involves many sequential, interrelated moving parts interacting over years.

To visualize your financial future, let's turn to an ancient model. Imagine the outline of a majestic Aztec pyramid as seen from a distance. Visualize the pyramid's size, its height, and width, including its visual totality and durability that spans centuries.

Keep that visual of the Aztec pyramid in mind.

Now let's look at the Aztec pyramid more carefully, paying attention to the details of its design. You might notice that Aztec pyramids have strong foundations and multiple levels that support heavy top tiers. Up close, you see how the pyramid is built to last, layer by layer. It is made *by increments.*

An Aztec pyramid serves as a good metaphor for financial security.

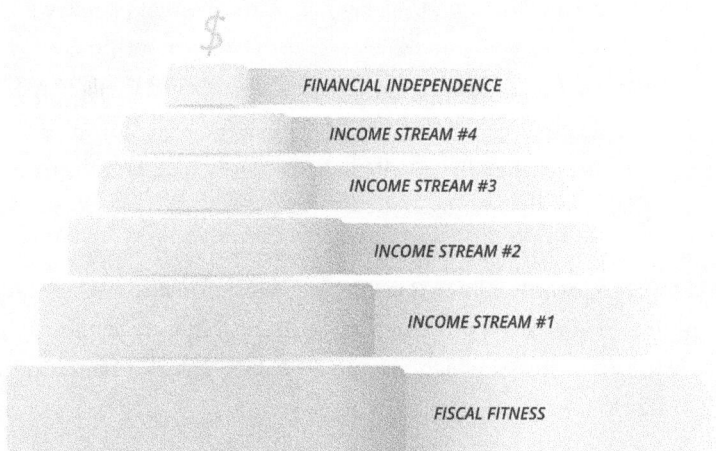

FINANCIAL INDEPENDENCE

INCOME STREAM #4

INCOME STREAM #3

INCOME STREAM #2

INCOME STREAM #1

FISCAL FITNESS

As you visualize your financial security, try to relate it to that mental picture of an Aztec pyramid. Your Life Plan will shape the size and design of the pyramid. Consider the materials, timeline, and everything required for you to construct an enduring structure.

Let's take an example. Suppose financial Independence is your long-term goal. Subordinate layers, each representing a specific financial target or period, would support this top tier goal. Your path to financial freedom might involve many steps, or just a few. For example:

Base: Eliminate debt and reduce high-cost structures

Tier 1: Increase savings

Tier 2: Secure one recurring passive revenue stream

Tier 3: Secure a second passive revenue stream

Tier 4: Secure a third passive revenue stream

Tier 5: Secure a fourth passive revenue stream

Tier 6: Improve tax-efficiencies and net cash flow, perhaps by reducing leverage

Top tier: Financial freedom

Visualizing the totality of your financial future, then incrementalize. Break down your goals into manageable, actionable steps. Create as many steps or tiers to your pyramid, as necessary to erect a structure that does not crumble—but also one you can climb in an acceptable time frame.

Stone by stone, tier-by-tier, build your financial future from the ground up. Start with a strong foundation. The first tiers are the hardest and most important; they ground and support the whole structure. Each level holds up the next.

Your focus at any point in time is the current tier under construction. Once that tier is in place, move on to the next one. You cannot sustain the top layers without secure, grounded lower layers.

In practice, building each tier may involve achieving multiple supporting financial goals every year.

That's where your Annual Financial Plan comes in. The Annual Financial Plan is your current year operating budget. It's how you monitor your financial progress month by month. To minimize the time required to maintain this plan, you can use a short-cut technique called Big Picture Budgeting.

BIG PICTURE BUDGETING

If you prioritize financial security, you must understand your money flows. Remember, in building financial security, we focus on cash. Measuring and monitoring your cash flow is vital. Your time is precious.

Conventional budgeting counts money each time you spend it. This can be too detailed and time-consuming for busy professionals and deters budgeting. Counting cappuccinos each week and then devising a quota for visiting Starbucks isn't a good use of time. It is tedious and unnecessary unless you live close to the margin.

Big Picture Budgeting provides a time-efficient view of your money flows. This technique is just as useful as traditional budgeting, but easier to maintain, because it tracks the money flows at a high level.

In the spirit of saving before spending, your annual financial formula will look like this:

MAXIMIZERS	FORMULA	MINIMIZERS
S = SAVINGS		T = TAXES
W = WAGES/EARNED INCOME	$S = W + P - T - R - D - C$	R = RECURRING
P = PASSIVE INCOME		FIXED EXPENSES
C = CONSUMPTION		D = DEBT

Here's what each element in that formula means.

MAXIMIZERS

Savings: The amount of money you tuck away every month/year.

Wages: The amount of money you earn from your time, including secondary jobs or side hustles.

Passive Income: The amount of money you earn in your sleep, the product of your savings and investments—the key to your enriched life.

Consumption: A unique spending category. Mathematically, you want to minimize consumption to increase savings. However, consumption delivers enjoyment and quality of life. It reflects that cappuccino habit as well as spending on restaurants, clothes, travel, entertainment, and other fun types of discretionary spending. By keeping consumption as a variable and maintaining savings as a fixed amount, you can balance between spending and saving.

MINIMIZERS

Taxes reflect all your various tax payments—including federal, state, and property taxes.

Recurring fixed expenses include mortgage/rent payments and aggregate household running costs (e.g., utilities, lawn care, association fees, car payments, tuition or student loans, insurance, any other debt servicing or regular, fixed payments).

Debt captures any other financial obligations you have not already reflected in recurring fixed costs.

The ENRICH methodology maximizes savings, passive income, and consumption. It minimizes recurring costs and taxes, and it eliminates debt so that wages/earned income become optional. That is complete financial Independence.

Understanding your broad money flows helps you drill down and manage recurring costs. Once you form a picture of the dollar movements, you can devise ways to maximize happy spending (savings and consumption) and minimize unhappy outflows (recurring costs and taxes).

The Big Picture Budget provides just enough detail for you to get a handle on money flows without overwhelming the budgeting process. Update and review the budget monthly.

The more detailed and time-consuming the budget, the less likely you will stick with it. It does not matter whether you spend money on cappuccinos or clothes, so long as total consumption spending tracks with your financial targets. This method allows you to monitor consumption expenditures in just a few line items. Big Picture Budgeting accounts for money as it leaves your bank account—such as when you pay the rent, pay a monthly credit card bill, or make an ATM cash withdrawal. It does not track every discrete purchase, such as the individual charges on a credit card bill or cash payments at the grocery store.

With this baseline consumption budget, you can create dedicated line items for any consumption category you want to monitor closely. For example, if you wish to granulate dining and travel costs, then you can dedicate line items to these particular categories. The budget should also track spending categories for which there might be tax deduction benefits, such as car and commuting costs and medical costs. This information will help you complete your tax returns.

The idea is to get just enough detail to monitor money flows without overburdening the process. As you perfect your budget, you can add or subtract detail based on your needs and goals.

This process requires buy-in at the family level with a consensus on annual total consumption expenditures. To maintain this family buy-in, it will help to involve your family in periodic reviews so that each family member feels they contribute to the family's financial freedom, while understanding the rationale and benefits of the financial goals.

HOW TO BUILD YOUR ANNUAL FINANCIAL PLAN

The Annual Financial Plan represents your or your family's economic plan for the year. The first part of the plan operates like a dashboard that projects your financial targets, income, and available consumption spending for the year.

Financial Targets: High-level summary of the year's financial goals. These goals directly tie to your Life Plan. Each year, you should move the goalpost toward your long-term financial priorities. Keep your financial objectives front and center and account for all income as well as taxes for the year.

Income: Project all earnings for the year, from all sources (earned income and passive income), after taxes. You may need to keep a separate P&L budget(s) for your passive investment activity.

Available Consumption Spending: Calculates net income, after taxes and after savings. It is the amount of total discretionary spending possible within the year, given your financial goals.

ANNUAL FAMILY BUDGET USING THE BIG PICTURE TECHNIQUE

FINANCIAL TARGETS: Target #1 for the year

Target #2 for the year

CONSOLIDATED BUDGET	PRIOR YEAR ACTUALS	MONTHLY	ANNUAL	JAN.	FEB.	...	TOTAL
INCOME							
EARNED INCOME:							
Salary #1							
Bonus/Commission							
Salary #2 (spouse)							
Bonus/Commission							
Earned Income - subtotal							
Less: Federal/State Taxes							
Less: Savings from Income							
Available for Consumption							
PASSIVE INCOME:							
Net Passive Income – Stream #1							
Income – Investment account #1							
Passive Income - subtotal							

The next section of the annual budget details your savings plan. Many people target a savings rate or a savings amount, then fall short because they did not specify where to direct their savings. Avoid that situation by indicating the account destination for your intended savings, in addition to the targeted amount. This helps you stay on course and monitor progress.

In calculating the year's target savings rate, remember you will have two sources of savings: a percentage of your earned income, and all of your passive income. By reinvesting all the passive income, you benefit from the power of compounding, which accelerates your financial security.

SAVINGS	PRIOR YEAR ACTUALS	MONTHLY	ANNUAL	JAN.	FEB.	...	TOTAL
IRA							
401(k)							
529 College							
Investment #1							
Total Savings							

Now we get to the focus of conventional budgets: consumption spending.

Spending Budget: Your projected expenses for the year. The household budget captures ALL spending outflows—recurring costs, consumption, debt—other than taxes and savings.

Identify the total amount of recurring fixed costs; usually, this number shocks people. That is why knowing your numbers is so integral to financial security. The total expenses should not exceed the amount available for consumption identified in the income section. When you create the annual budget target, these numbers must agree with each other.

SPENDING	PRIOR YEAR ACTUALS	MONTHLY	ANNUAL	JAN.	FEB.	...	TOTAL
RECURRING/FIXED COSTS							
Mortgage/Rent							
Child care							
Utilities							
HOA							
Insurance							
House							
Car							
Health							
Life							
Car/Transportation							
Tuition							
Club Membership							
Recurring Costs - subtotal							
CONSUMPTION							
ATM/Cash Withdrawal							
Credit Card #1							
Credit Card #2							
Medical							
Travel							
Charity							
Consumption - subtotal							
Total Spending							

Variance Tracking: This calculates your cumulative year-to-date actual spending vs. your aggregate year-to-date budgeted expenditures. Calculating the monthly variance, positive or negative, shows you how well you are sticking to your plans and whether you need a mid-course correction. Keep in mind most spending is lumpy. Some months may produce a positive variance, some months an unfavorable variance. What should concern you is the cumulative effect.

VARIANCES	PRIOR YEAR ACTUALS	MONTHLY	ANNUAL	JAN.	FEB.	...	TOTAL
Cumulative YTD Actual Income							
Cumulative YTD Actual Spending							
Cumulative Variance							
Cumulative YTD Budgeted Savings							
Cumulative YTD Actual Savings							
Cumulative Variance							

INSIGHTS

After Big Picture Budgeting, I discovered that my family's lifestyle—our consumption—represented just one-third of earned income. That meant two-thirds of my hard-earned paycheck went toward servicing a high-cost structure (we lived in one of the world's most expensive cities while I worked) and taxes.

By rethinking a costly structure and relying on tax-efficient investments, we maintained our lifestyle with a whole lot less income. We were able to lower the hurdle rate for our financial freedom, even after earmarking a buffer. As discussed in chapter 6, the 80 percent replacement income recommended by Fidelity and other financial advisors proved unnecessary. This revelation accelerated our financial freedom by years.

This lower hurdle rate, of course, required geographic flexibility. Once work became optional, we were able to move to a high-quality but lower-cost location without factoring in employment considerations.

After you calculate savings, taxes, recurring costs, and consumption money flows, the following guidelines will help fine-tune your financial performance:

- **⑤** *Debt.* Unless there is a tax advantage, eliminating debt should be your number one financial goal after you establish an emergency cushion. All credit card and consumer debt should go. If you cannot pay for something in cash, rethink the purchase. You will never build real financial security if you pay a bank's interest before you pay yourself. Tax-deductible mortgage interest is a judgment call. In many expensive real estate markets, it is often cheaper to rent than to own.
- **⑤** *Recurring cost structure.* For many professionals, streamlining recurring costs requires the most focus. Your fixed cost structure needs to scale way below your income. The fixed costs should account for a third of your net earnings or less if you want sufficient cushion to maximize savings and consumption. If your cost structure matches your income, you are committing yourself to the high-income treadmill...it never stops.

Scaling down your cost structure may require some tough decisions, like opting for a smaller house with lower upkeep expenses. *The smaller your lifestyle footprint, the lower the hurdle for financial security.* It's math. That is the economic trade-off.

You may want to drill down into your recurring costs to identify which ongoing financial commitments are essential and which are not. Identify the recurring expenses that bring joy and pleasure; eliminate or minimize those that do not. Be ruthless. Cut anything that does not produce repeated satisfaction or usage, including assessing the utility of club/gym memberships and subscriptions.

Above all, watch out for lifestyle creep. It sneaks up on you. Recall the nine tenets of fiscal fitness from chapter 6. Living below your means is part and parcel with creating financial security.

THE COMMITMENT

Financial planning only works when you stick with it. Devise and commit to a system you can support long term, and to which you can dedicate some time each month. There are no shortcuts, and simple is best. Measuring and monitoring your financial health, and knowing your numbers are crucial to financial security. This often becomes an enjoyable process as you progress toward your financial targets.

There are some fintech tools, such as Mint and Personal Capital, and various apps to support budgeting and monitor spending. Creating your own Excel sheet may be worth the effort; just don't get lost in the weeds and miss the big picture.

Finally, be sure to start with realistic goals. Often people get into quicksand and give up too early because the targets are too far out of reach. Also, carefully consider timing. Sometimes it is just not the right time to tackle an ambitious goal given competing or higher priorities. Often, it takes longer than you expect to hit some targets. Focus on what you can realistically achieve. As the saying goes, a bird in the hand is worth two in the bush.

ENRICH: KEY TAKEAWAYS: BUILD YOUR FINANCIAL SECURITY

Want to double your chances of achieving financial security? Make a financial plan. Approach financial planning the way you would any other ambitious goal. The following Take Action exercises guide you through each step of building your financial plans. This process takes commitment, but the payoff—financial security—is worth the time investment.

⑤ Written financial goals double the probability of success.

- An Aztec pyramid is a useful financial planning metaphor: visualize, then incrementalize.
- The Annual Financial Plan (AFP) is an operating plan that bridges the present to your long-term financial targets.
- Big Picture Budgeting is a short-cut technique that spotlights the key drivers and saves you time.

So far, we have progressed from *theory* to *goals* to *planning*. Financial planning keeps you on track with your financial goals, just as life planning keeps you on track with your life goals. Both planning processes underpin the ENRICH method of creating wealth in time, money, and meaning.

We're at the point where you have the knowledge and the tools to Reach for your most meaningful goals. Now it's time to start *doing*. In the next ENRICH step, you'll discover how to "Ignite" these plans in your everyday life.

ENRICH: TAKE ACTION: BUILD YOUR FINANCIAL SECURITY

This thirteen-step sequence guides you to plot your path toward financial security by identifying congruent short-, medium-, and long-term financial objectives. In short, you will build your own Aztec pyramid of financial security. The objectives you develop in this exercise plug directly into the financial section of your Life Plan.

1. Adopt the same time horizon and milestones as your Life Plan. Ten Years is usually a reasonable time frame. For a ten-year horizon, marking milestones at Year One, Year Five, and Year Ten is appropriate. This is the financial planning equivalent of an Aztec pyramid with three tiers.

2. Visualize. Plan with the end in sight. Identify the top tier on your targeted pyramid—Year Ten in this example.

3. Incrementalize. Working backward, identify and quantify the intermediate milestone (Year Five in this example). In order to reach the top tier, what do you need to accomplish for this intermediate marker? Use the goal-setting methods in chapter 4 to plot a milestone that supports achieving the long-term goal.

4. Incrementalize again. Working backward from the intermediate milestone, plot the current year goals. The Annual Financial Plan will capture these short-term goals.

5. Think through all the steps and outcomes required to hit each interval. Focus on the steps that need concentrated and sustained effort.

6. Do the math. Be realistic. The goals for each milestone/tier should be ambitious but not impossible to achieve. Incrementally build on progress, tier by tier. Be sure to consider the power of compounding.

7. Check for sanity: Consider each goal individually and collectively. Are these goals possible or impossible?

8. Stress-test: If an exogenous event happens, how will you adjust your plan? How fragile is your plan?

9. Ensure alignment between all the financial goals across this time horizon.

10. Motivation: What drives these goals, and how will they enrich your life? List at least three positive consequences of realizing these financial goals. What implications would arise from inaction?

11. Schedule quarterly performance reviews to track progress toward long-term financial goals. Set calendar alerts to remind you of these performance reviews.

12. Schedule the date you will begin next year's annual planning process.

13. Implement some tools from chapter 9 to increase your probability of success and maintain momentum.

ENRICH: TAKE ACTION: BUILD YOUR
ANNUAL FINANCIAL PLAN

This is your operating budget for the current year. Using the Big Picture Budgeting technique, follow these systematic considerations to formulate your annual plan. Here is the complete template. You can access a free soft copy of this template at www.enrich101.com.

ANNUAL FAMILY BUDGET USING THE BIG PICTURE TECHNIQUE

FINANCIAL TARGETS: Target #1 for the year _____

Target #2 for the year _____

CONSOLIDATED BUDGET	PRIOR YEAR ACTUALS	MONTHLY	ANNUAL	JAN.	FEB.	...	TOTAL
INCOME							
EARNED INCOME:							
Salary #1							
Bonus/Commission							
Salary #2 (spouse)							
Bonus/Commission							
Earned Income - subtotal							
Less: Federal/State Taxes							
Less: Savings from Income							
Available for Consumption							
PASSIVE INCOME:							
Net Passive Income – Stream #1							
Income – Investment account #1							
Passive Income - subtotal							
SAVINGS	PRIOR YEAR ACTUALS	MONTHLY	ANNUAL	JAN.	FEB.	...	TOTAL
IRA							
401(k)							
529 College							
Investment #1							
Total Savings							

SPENDING	PRIOR YEAR ACTUALS	MONTHLY	ANNUAL	JAN.	FEB.	...	TOTAL
RECURRING/FIXED COSTS							
Mortgage/Rent							
Child care							
Utilities							
HOA							
Insurance							
House							
Car							
Health							
Life							
Car/Transportation							
Tuition							
Club Membership							
Recurring Costs - subtotal							
CONSUMPTION							
ATM/Cash Withdrawal							
Credit Card #1							
Credit Card #2							
Medical							
Travel							
Charity							
Consumption - subtotal							
Total Spending							

VARIANCES	PRIOR YEAR ACTUALS	MONTHLY	ANNUAL	JAN.	FEB.	...	TOTAL
Cumulative YTD Actual Income							
Cumulative YTD Actual Spending							
Cumulative Variance							
Cumulative YTD Budgeted Savings							
Cumulative YTD Actual Savings							
Cumulative Variance							

1. Decide on the format and the cycle (calendar, birthday, or fiscal year) to build and sustain your financial plan. Excel is a recommended format, and you can create a new tab for each new plan year.

2. Calculate projected income by consolidating income from all sources and deducting hypothetical taxes.

3. Identify the year's savings target and the destinations for your savings dollars, by account. Create specific line items and track each savings destination (where the savings will go). Destinations might include IRA, 401(k) or 529 accounts, investment accounts, the purchase of real estate, or the reduction of debt. This destination specificity for your savings dollars helps you stay on track throughout the year.

4. Calculate Available Income for Consumption. Deduct taxes and savings to get net income.

5. Create a personal or household budget, by month, based on the Available Consumption Spending. Use the Big Picture technique to capture all the critical categories, including wages/earned income, passive income, savings/investment, recurring costs, debt, and consumption. Identify any specific consumption expenses you want to granulate, and create a line item for each consumption category you will monitor and control. The amount of detail in this budget depends upon your particular situation and goals. Just make sure you capture and categorize ALL spending, in the most time-efficient way, without overburdening the process.

6. Calculate Net Passive Income by source. Create line item(s) for each passive income source, such as a taxable investment account or real estate property, and calculate the net income of each. Most brokerage firms will provide estimated cash flows in your monthly statements. Crucially, always think net income after taxes, and account for tax-beneficial revenue (such as municipal bonds and real estate).

7. Check for sanity: Does all the budgeted spending for a year fit within the available discretionary spending? Will your budgeted savings rate keep you on track toward long-term financial targets? Are the numbers conservative and realistic, or optimistic?

8. Add some fun: Provide for some enjoyment. Otherwise, this process becomes a real slog, or worse, you abandon the program altogether. Set aside some money to make the year fun, enough to provide something to look forward to. These little things make the journey more comfortable and help you stay on track long term.

9. Stress-test your plan. Can you cope if income falls by 10 percent? If income falls by 20 percent or more, are you able to restructure recurring expenses?

10. Pick a consistent time each month to update and review your activity and track progress. Set calendar alerts to remind you of these performance reviews.

11. Calculate monthly and cumulative variances for income, savings, and spending. Take corrective action as appropriate to maintain the integrity of your financial targets.

12. Make sure you receive and review financial statements each month for each bank, credit card, and investment account you own.

13. Implement some tools from chapter 9 to increase your chances of success and maintain momentum.

STEP IV

IGNITE

Congratulations. By now, you have formulated your Mission Statement and Hierarchy of Priorities and may have conceptualized some life and financial aspirations. If you are an overachiever—and if you're reading this book, you probably are—you may have even created your Life Plan and Annual Financial Plan.

We have explored how creating compelling goals through visualization and incrementalization vastly improves the probability of success. However, plans alone will not get you to the Promised Land. How can you convert these plans into action and reality?

The fourth ENRICH step Ignites your aspirations and plans.

ESSENTIALIZE **E** NARROW **N** REACH **R** IGNITE **I** CALIBRATE **C** HARNESS TIME **H**

Sustained and successful goal attainment demands a systematic approach. This chapter offers actionable strategies to generate momentum. It also outlines techniques for overcoming obstacles—the fear factor and present bias—to getting started.

Let's get going.

CHAPTER 9

——

GET INTO ACTION

"The secret of getting ahead is getting started."

—MARK TWAIN

"You miss 100 percent of the shots you don't take."

—WAYNE GRETZKY

I hopped on my bike and started pedaling, wobbly but mechanically, ten miles in the wrong direction. No sentiment, no emotion. Just the lingering anxiety that comes at the beginning of any great journey. "Could I? Should I? Would I?" I wondered.

I embarked on a solo and self-supported expedition that ultimately spanned 3,600 miles, cycling from Lisbon, the westernmost part of continental Europe, to Istanbul, the crossroads of Asia. On that quiet Sunday morning, navigating out of Portugal's cobblestone capital was my foremost concern. My focus that day—my single modest goal—was to find a rideable road to the city of Santarem, around fifty miles northeast of Lisbon. As I wrote at the time:

> How I get from the heart of Lisbon to Santarem is up to the imagination, and my ability to find the N10 secondary road.

That's the road with the fine squiggly yellow line on my giant map of the country. In short, I am winging it. I don't even know where I will sleep, but I have 14 hours of daylight to figure that out.

Istanbul was far-removed from my thinking that day, and most days until the very end of the expedition. The journey's start was anything but promising. In the first three days, the Portuguese police busted me for cycling on a so-called highway. I lost direction on unmarked and secondary roads that snaked through desolate comatose towns. I fought unreliable GPS, debilitating headwinds, and dehydration. If getting to Istanbul were the focus, I would have likely given up in that first week. It would have seemed too far, too hard, and too daunting. Getting to Istanbul was a future problem.

The task I faced each day was immediate and actionable. If I could not make it to the next significant town, then Istanbul would be out of the question. Each day I focused intently on what I needed to do *that* day. Could I get to the next major town? Yes. That was within my control.

Increment by increment, I progressed across sixteen countries, traversing the Pyrenees, Alps, Balkans, and many other obstacles. Some days, the milestones were big. When the going got tough, the goals got micro, such as cycling for another mile or getting to the next intersection. (Cycling across France, the goal was usually to get to the next patisserie.) I adjusted the milestones to keep moving forward while ensuring that I could and would always get to the next marker.

Eighty cycling days after that wobbly start in Portugal, I found myself in Istanbul, having pedaled across a continent to get there.

My bike ride across Europe was nothing more than a series of day rides connected by a coherent plan. By stringing together these small micro-goals, I crossed a continent.

While cycling across Europe was a monumental experience, it was also just one milestone in my extended quest to eventually cycle around the world, one continent at a time.

SET UP FOR SUCCESS

Creating an enriched life can be complicated and messy. Let's face it: getting started is *hard*. According to research by the Association for Training Development, there is only a 10 percent probability of actualizing a goal that is just an idea. Give yourself a break. Create the conditions to succeed.

What is the difference between an idea and a goal?

A piece of paper.

The first step to achieving a compelling goal is to put it on paper. Make it tactile, make it real, and make it visible. An idea on paper has significantly more gravitas and Impact than one in your head.

In a 2015 study on goal achievement, Gail Matthews discovered that those who wrote down their goals accomplished 50 percent more than those who did not. Mathews is a psychologist at the Dominican University of California. This practice of writing down goals is another common trait of high-performance individuals. It's no coincidence that both world-record adventurers profiled in chapter 4 *religiously write down* goals.

When you write down your goals, also identify the motive for each one, the Why. As we also discussed in chapter 4, this is where authenticity comes in. How does this goal support your enriched life? How does it align with your priorities? Understanding the reason you want to accomplish something provides inspiration and motivation and ensures continued commitment. *Writing* that reason down has even more power.

Managing goals electronically (such as in Excel or Word documents) can also be useful, provided you also print out the documents. One trick is to make one of your goals your password for all things electronic. This keeps your goal top-of-mind throughout the day. As a bonus, you improve internet security when you move on to the next goal and change your password accordingly.

ACTION!

Writing down goals is a great start, but staring at a list of goals or a Life Plan can disorient and even paralyze—especially when it's on paper. Starting anything new is intimidating, forbidding. Inertia is a powerful force to conquer. So how to get into action?

The way to begin an audacious ambition is to mimic an infant learning to walk.

To start on something big, take a baby step.

This baby step—something you can accomplish within one day, or even a few hours—is the second most important thing you can do to get started after writing down the goal. Give yourself a quick win and move the goalpost forward just a wee bit. That is all it takes to start. When making that baby step, purge all thoughts of the end goal and the magnitude of the total task, just as I did when cycling across Europe. Focus only on what you have to do NOW and NEXT. This applies to any kind of goal you pursue—including goals from your Life Plan, Life List, and Annual Financial Plan.

Below are some actionable strategies for taking that first step.

INCREMENTALIZE

Plan big but act small. Break down an audacious goal into a series of manageable micro-goals. Focus wholeheartedly on the immediate next milestone you can achieve. Recall that even on Everest Summit Day, Annabelle Bond focused on three intermediate goals before turning her attention to the peak.

SPECIFICITY

We previously discussed SMARTA (Specific, Measurable, Accountable, Realistic, Timely, Authentic) goals. The more vivid the SMARTA goal, the easier it is to get started. Addressing the what, when, where, how, and why requires thinking through the detail. This demystifies the task.

Suppose improved fitness is your goal. "Exercise more, get fit, and go to the gym" are popular but ineffective goals. No call to action exists because these aspirations lack specificity. To start a new exercise regimen, you might decide the time you will go to the gym. Research and identify the specific workout you will follow. Review the individual exercises. Pack your gym bag; set your alarm. By thinking through the details, you create the conditions to follow through, so that getting up and going to the gym becomes a reflex response.

IMMERSE YOURSELF

Surround yourself with people who have done, or who are doing, what you seek to accomplish. Do not be shy about reaching out to like-minded people. The more sustained effort a goal requires, the more the experiences of others will provide you with motivation, inspiration, knowledge, and confidence.

Before I started the Euro cycle, I surrounded myself with experts. Mark Beaumont, who broke the world record for circumnavigating the world by bike, and Rob Lilwall, who cycled home to London from Siberia the long way via Australia, inspired me. I spent time with these and other ultra long-distance cyclists, picked their brains, and stayed in touch. I read their books and their friends' books. Physically and virtually connecting with these accomplished cyclists boosted my motivation and confidence levels, and greatly magnified my determination to do my thing.

CREATE A CATALYST

Do something to jumpstart the process. It might be a workshop, retreat, or event that gives you the skills and confidence to get going. For a catalyst to become a commitment, it has to be in the calendar. Putting money on the line (i.e., paying for a workshop) increases the commitment level. For the Euro cycle, I purchased a nonrefundable one-way ticket to Lisbon early in the planning process. I committed.

REHEARSE THE BEGINNING

Organize a trial or partial run, so the unfamiliar becomes familiar. Rehearsing builds confidence and lowers the intimidation factor. The day before starting my Euro challenge, I did a practice ride to the *Praca de Commercio*, the majestic square where, the next morning, I set off on the expedition.

NO FANFARE, NO FUSS

Sometimes we make big starts bigger than they need to be, and this increases the fear factor. I have cycled across two continents; both journeys had humble beginnings. You can and should make it a big deal when you reach your endpoint. But it's often best to have a simple, practical, low-key start that will simply get you to the next increment.

SUMMON MOTIVATION SPARKS

Recall the Why and the Why Not. Reflect on why you want to accomplish this goal and the consequences of inaction. This can provide powerful motivational sparks. Visualizing the colorful details of a successful outcome—for example, when I get into shape, I will fit into my favorite swimsuit by June—can provide a motivating spark.

THE PROMISED LAND

With your second baby step, you begin to create momentum. "It does not matter how slowly you go as long as you do not stop," Confucius counseled. Willpower alone will not power you to the finish line. You need momentum. These eleven techniques help generate propulsion toward the Promised Land:

1. Integrate; Don't Segregate
2. Add Accountability
3. Schedule, Create Reminders and Visual Cues
4. Impose Deadlines
5. Go Public and Social
6. Focus on What You Can Control
7. Aim for Consistency, Not Perfection
8. Get Some Gratification

9. Why and Why Not
10. Measure and Monitor
11. Mix It Up

1. INTEGRATE, DON'T SEGREGATE

A catalyst is a great tool to jump-start a goal-directed effort. However, for long-term success, integrate the goal-oriented activity into your daily life to ensure a favorable outcome. The better the activity fits into your regular schedule, the better the chance of achievement.

Why do most diets fail? Because they're temporary aberrations from normal life. When the diet ends and normalcy returns, weight gain reappears viciously as the habits and benefits from the diet recede. For this reason, Weight Watchers has become a multibillion-dollar business based on making dieting a lifestyle and not a project.

2. ADD ACCOUNTABILITY

Planning increases your chances of hitting a goal by 50 percent. Want to improve your chances by 65 percent? Get an accountability partner. Commit to someone whom you respect.

Want to boost your success chances up to 95 percent? Have regular, specific accountability appointments with the person to whom you have committed. These astounding benefits of accountability derive from research by the Association for Talent Development.

According to research by psychologist Gail Matthews, weekly written progress reports have a similar positive uplift toward goal success. They almost double the chances of goal achievement.

3. GO PUBLIC AND SOCIAL

Another way to improve your ability to hit a goal is to commit publicly, such as by posting and periodically updating on social media. The more you connect with other people or communities working toward the same goal, the more likely you are to stay on the bandwagon. We are a social species. Surround yourself with people who share your passions and aspirations.

Friendly competition and collaboration motivate. Figuring out a way (even virtually) to make the journey with someone else helps you maintain motivation and pulls you through the rough patches. This holds especially true for fitness and health goals but applies to practically any objective. Through online forums and communities, find groups or individuals working toward the same outcome as you. Do not go it alone. In whatever tribe you belong to, there is someone, somewhere, who shares your aspiration. Find him or her. You will vastly improve the odds of success.

4. FOCUS ON WHAT YOU CAN CONTROL

There might be numerous potholes and opportunities for things to go wrong. Circumstances beyond your control can distract and discourage. Identify and mitigate the obstacles, of course. That is proper planning. But do not permit these issues to derail you. Controlling the factors is within your power to control and filter out the distractions.

5. AIM FOR CONSISTENCY, NOT PERFECTION

Research suggests these three factors can help you foster a good habit or break a bad one:

- Commit to at least thirty days (sometimes it takes up to ninety days)
- Make it daily
- Start simple

There will be some days you just won't feel like it. You can give yourself a short break or go easier, but consistency matters.

6. SCHEDULE, CREATE REMINDERS AND VISUAL CUES

In addition to writing down goals, schedule the recurring time you will dedicate to advancing each goal. A commitment is not a commitment until it's in the calendar. Scheduling is vital to avoid the default setting. We schedule times for meetings, conference calls, dentist appointments, and visits from the plumber. Why would we relegate our goals to an inferior status? In fact, when we're managing the calendar, inviolate time for our priority goals should precede other commitments.

Place subtle, visual reminders of your intentions in places where you'll encounter them during your daily routines. For example, place sticky notes in your bathroom or, for a fitness goal, put a packed gym bag by your front door. Be sure to activate calendar reminders as well.

7. IMPOSE DEADLINES

The longer the goal horizon, the more intermediate milestones are needed (more urgently and in greater number) to push you to the finish line. Deadlines, even artificially self-imposed ones, have a remarkable effect on sharpening and compressing effort. If you create an artificial deadline, treat it as real. Put it in the calendar.

8. GET SOME GRATIFICATION

Celebrate the milestones and wins and have some fun NOW. As I pedaled across Europe, I kept looking forward to the next small victory celebration; it propelled me. My celebrations—which happened at least once a day—usually involved visiting gelato shops. (Burning thousands of calories daily meant not having to count them.)

Getting started and keeping going is easier when the incremental steps are small, and the quick wins celebrated. One effective form of calorie-free gratification is to receive acknowledgment and encouragement from others. This acknowledgment functions like steroids and substantially boosts motivation.

9. WHY AND WHY NOT

Regularly remind yourself of the rationale for your endeavor. Sometimes pull strategies work best: how will I benefit? Sometimes push strategies work best: what's the downside of inaction? Switch the pull and push strategies over time, if necessary, to keep things exciting and varied.

In the last week of my Euro cycle, I hit a nasty, punishing weather system that tested my resolve—even though I was nearly at the finish line. Unrelenting wind, rain, and cold, as well as fatigue and isolation, depleted my energy and spirit. I had to dig deep to keep going. I pictured the disappointment I'd see on my son's face if I quit. I thought of the hopeful children whose charity I was pedaling for, and how much money was on the line *for them*. I found the strength to power through, because of The Why.

10. MEASURE AND MONITOR

Quantify and measure your progress toward each increment.

Whatever you tackle, devise a way to measure your advancement. Schedule and put into your calendar regular review periods to assess your progress. In these reviews, identify what works and how to optimize your efforts going forward.

Let's take weight loss again as an example. Research shows that people who measure (by weighing regularly) and monitor (by moderating dietary intake) are most likely to reach their weight loss goals.

Measuring your progress also comes with a bonus. Research shows that making progress toward your goals improves well-being and increases happiness. Put another way, measuring progress toward a SMARTA goal produces a multiplier effect that gets you closer to the supreme goal of an enriched life. That is a bang for the buck!

11. MIX IT UP

Consider mixing up your activities to keep the endeavor fresh and compelling. There are many strategies in this chapter's tool kit to help you keep going. You do not have to use all of these. Select a few and stick with them. You can and should alternate methods over time. Interjecting variety is itself an effective strategy to maintain momentum.

These strategies help you Ignite and keep going. But what about overcoming the *psychological* gravity that can deter ignition?

OVERCOME GRAVITY

Let's unpack two "gravitational" forces that can keep you from getting into action:

1. THE FEAR FACTOR

Sometimes there are real external obstacles in your way. But chances are the biggest obstacles to getting started or to making progress will be those in your head. We often plunge ourselves into mental quicksand, which results in inertia.

Fear results from a stressful trigger that can paralyze as well as energize. Rejection, failure, uncertainty, embarrassment, and change intimidate us. Fear is healthy and natural. You should be worried if you do *not* have anxieties as you aspire toward enrichment.

We usually spend too much time thinking about what could go wrong, rather than thinking about how to improve the odds of success. Thinking through ways to ensure success or limit the fallout of failure reduces the stress stimuli and the fear factor.

Some fears may persist and are entirely rational and justified. The best way to deal with anxiety is to do so analytically. Do the math. Get the thoughts out of your head. The more you let insecurities fester, the more they paralyze your progress. Refer to the Take Action exercise below for a systematic process to conquer the fear factor.

By approaching fear mathematically, you can simplify, clarify, and make a more objective and informed decision on the merits of action or inaction. In going through this process, you will likely discover that your anxieties are overblown. Often, the advantages of action outweigh the downside, especially with mitigators in place. If you calculate that the downside poses too much risk, you can be confident in your decision. You can make peace and move on. Either way, the analysis provides a benefit.

This fear-solving process applies to almost any circumstance, big or small. Are you worried about the risks of a mid-career change, or taking a sabbatical? Do the math. Are you fearful of asking out the spinning instructor at the gym? Again, do the math.

2. PRESENT BIAS

We think short term. Corporate America thinks in quarters. Attention spans measure in seconds. In an always-on world, we expect immediate gratification. That makes it hard to action a goal that does not produce an immediate payoff.

Let's turn to marshmallows to illustrate this point. The famous Stanford experiments in the late 1960s tempted children with those sugary confections. Children could get one marsh-mallow now or two in fifteen minutes. The fancy term for present bias is hyperbolic discounting—choosing a smaller reward today over a more substantial reward tomorrow. In follow-up research, the children from the marshmallow study who delayed gratification tended to have better life outcomes in terms of factors, such as educational attainment and body mass index. Academic studies link discipline to achievement across varied domains, including personal finance, fitness, and job performance.

This marshmallow research has been replicated using a variety of rewards, including money, and with various age groups, including adults. The outcome preferences for immediate gratification are similar. This explains why saving for retirement challenges many. Thinking about the future is hard, and working toward the future is even harder. It's like going to heaven. Everyone wants to get there, but no one wants to make the trip.

So what to do?

A proven way to overcome hyperbolic discounting is to reverse engineer incentives. This involves looking ahead, calculating the present value, and then constructing a positive or negative stimulus around that present value. A positive incentive might be some kind of personal reward for taking action toward your goal. Negative incentives, such as contributing to a cause counter to your values, can also motivate well. Suppose your goal is to save a certain amount of money within a specified period. You promise yourself you will start saving next week. Next week then becomes next month, a classic example of hyperbolic discounting. You can overcome this by calculating the opportunity cost, which is the amount of interest you forfeit by not saving now. You commit to donating this amount to a cause that annoys you. Online tools such as stickK.com can help you put dollars on the line to help you commit and achieve any goal.

SUSTAINING A MULTI-YEAR GOAL

Airin Zainul, an accomplished Malaysian media executive, employed many techniques in a sustained five-year quest to run the World Marathon Majors before turning forty-five. The World Marathon Majors is the running world's "Grand Slam." The Majors involve the world's six most prestigious marathons—London, Tokyo, New York, Chicago, Berlin, and Boston. Remarkably, Zainul does not consider herself a natural runner. "I am a late bloomer," she confesses. "I only seriously picked up running in 2012, and it was at the time a stress-reliever and a way to lose weight."

To achieve her five-year goal, Zainul used most of the techniques identified in this chapter. She:

- Integrated training into her daily life by focusing on early-morning or late-night long-distance runs to minimize the Impact on her various roles—as executive, mom, wife, and daughter. "It's all meshed in," she says.
- Aimed for consistency, not perfection. "There are days when the mind wants to run, but the body is not willing," she laments.
- Used the Nike Running app to schedule her training and mileage targets, and to measure and monitor her progress.
- Created reminders and visual cues by drawing up a timeline board and penciling in dates on paper. "To visualize the end goal is vital," she testifies.
- Imposed a deadline to achieve the goal before her forty-fifth birthday.
- Made it social with a weekly running group. This kept her spirits up.
- Got competitive. "The beauty of marathon races," she says, "is that you run the same course as the 'elite' or world's best. Timing may be the determining factor, but there's no other sport that allows you to run on the same course, the same distance with the world's best."
- Put money on the line by spending considerable sums on race entry fees and logistics.
- Always reminded herself of The Why and Why Not. While running, she had lots of time to reflect on the reasons for this goal. This purpose—The Why—pulled her through the later, more challenging marathons.

A big dose of planfulness increases the probability of success. Zainul professes some sound advice about pursuing a multi-year goal:

Once the goal is in place, having a plan is critical in noting the timelines and milestones I need to achieve the target. With marathons, especially the World Majors, the dates of the races are always fixed. Therefore, planning your life, work, and family depends on those dates. Budgets also play a huge determining factor on which race to take on next. So drawing up a plan (much like a business plan), budgets and timelines are essential. It must all be documented so that the planning can take place. Apart from the "administrative" side of goal setting, training and keeping to schedule(s) are pertinent to ensure enough conditioning and mileage is achieved. Having to look at your whole calendar year and plotting the dates and milestones is a vital tool to ensure being on track. Always check and balance between work commitments and personal goals; make time for your family and friends.

Over the five years, did Zainul ever think about giving up? "It wasn't about giving up on the overall main goal," she tells me, "as I wanted to achieve 'something' before turning forty-five." She continued:

The thought of "giving up" occurred more during the training when having to run specific mileage weekly/monthly. On those days/weeks of not wanting to do the set/required distance, I would give myself a break and not do the runs. Usually, after some time off, I would get back on track after having the feeling of missing the running. It was a constant battle with myself.

ENRICH: KEY TAKEAWAYS: GET INTO ACTION

In this chapter, we've explored how to take that first step toward a big-ass goal. Goal attainment requires a mix of strategies to get going and to succeed. To Ignite any big goal, set yourself up for success and incrementalize for quick wins to build momentum, as I did pedaling across Europe. Then integrate these goals into daily life to maintain momentum, as Airin Zainul did on her five-year quest. These strategies work for any kind of endeavor—including work, personal, family, fitness, and financial goals. If you do not succeed at first, try another of the strategies in this chapter. Sometimes a change in tactic does the trick; experiment and tweak. Do not give up.

- Create the conditions to succeed: write down and schedule your goals.
- Take a baby step to Ignite a big goal and overcome inertia.
- Concentrate only on what you have to do Now and Next.
- Mix up the strategies to maintain momentum.
- Deal with fear rationally and analytically.
- Overcome present bias by using positive or negative incentives.

Igniting a goal with action empowers, gratifies, and enriches your life. The following two Take Action exercises will help you get into action.

ENRICH: TAKE ACTION: GET INTO ACTION

Identify a Life Plan goal you want to advance toward. Alternatively, you can build upon the exercise from chapter 4, Convert Priority to Goal.

1. Set up for success. Write the goal down, schedule it, and make it visible. Identify why the goal is essential to you.

2. Visualize. Plan big using SMARTA principles. To Ignite, get highly specific. Visualize the particular action of working toward this goal. Address the what, when, where, how, and why. If the target requires

preparation and planning, start now. Right now. Spend fifteen minutes to get into the mindset to achieve this goal. Do not stop until you write down the what, when, where, how, and why.

3. Incrementalize. Act small. Deconstruct the goal into manageable, achievable steps. It does not matter how many or how small the milestones are. The point is to get moving and advance the goalpost.

4. Identify the first baby step you can take in no more than a day. Then identify the second baby step.

5. Create conditions to succeed. Which strategies will you use to get started, and to maintain momentum? What do you need to do to activate these techniques?

6. Now commit: When are you going to take that first baby step?

7. Recall the Why.

8. Identify how you will overcome present bias. Which positive or negative incentives will motivate you to get into action?

9. Ignite!

ENRICH: TAKE ACTION: VANQUISH THE FEAR FACTOR

Identify a concern that might prevent you from moving forward on the goal you identified in the previous exercise. These seven steps will help you conquer the fear factor:

1. Pinpoint the fear. Write it down. Be as specific as possible.

2. On the same piece of paper, write down the advantages of taking action. What does success look like? How are you better off because of taking action? Ascribe a numerical value to success, say on a scale of 0 to 3.

3. Identify the consequences of inaction, of the status quo. Again, ascribe a numerical value of -3 to +3.

4. Take a reality check. Are these fears realistic? Have you correctly identified the advantages of action and the consequences of inaction?

5. Now ask: What is the worst case? What is the downside if your fear materializes? Ascribe a value -3 to +3.

6. Identify risk mitigators. What can you do to preclude or minimize the downside of failure? How realistic and achievable are these mitigators? Are they within your control? Ascribe a value 0 to +3.

7. Improve the odds. What can you do to increase the probability of success? Ascribe a value 0 to +3.

8. Do the math to arrive at a decision. The formula looks like this:

   Advantages of Action
   + Consequences of inaction
   – Potential downsides of action
   + Mitigators
   + Success factors
   = Decision to take action/inaction

9. Here is a real-world example, based on an elite professional's fear of not being prepared to retire early-ish at age fifty-five:

Advantages of early retirement:	+3
Consequences of inaction:	+1 (has to keep working)
Worst Case:	1 (has to keep working)
Mitigators:	+1 (100 percent control over savings and family spending)
Success Factors:	+1 (use tax-efficient investments)
Decision: Take Action/Inaction:	+5 (Go for It!!)

Overwhelmingly, the math supports prioritizing early-ish retirement at age fifty-five, and concentrating on all the financial levers within this person's control, to ensure success.

STEP V

—

CALIBRATE

Would you make better or different career decisions if you took money out of the equation?

Which habits enrich happiness?

Good gracious, what do Super Chickens have to do with your career?

In this journey to create wealth in time, money, and meaning, we've identified what matters most. We've set goals, established plans, and Ignited those plans. To Calibrate is to adjust and check for accuracy. In this part of the journey, we fine-tune the professional and the personal to maximize life satisfaction.

Calibrate, the fifth ENRICH step, helps you savor life's deliciousness at work and home.

ESSENTIALIZE **E** NARROW **N** REACH **R** IGNITE **I** CALIBRATE **C** HARNESS TIME **H**

Chapter 10 champions strategies to enrich your career. Taking money out of the equation (*Really?* you probably wonder) and innovating your career arc are two counterintuitive tactics, but they're your way out of the chicken coop.

Chapter 11 mixes conventional with unconventional thinking to survey happiness habits. Techniques include practicing the Five Ds, investing in the Essentials (which we first encountered in chapter 2), and discovering your Discomfort Zone.

CHAPTER 10

———

BUST OUT OF THE CHICKEN COOP

"Success is not the key to happiness. Happiness is the key to success. If you love what you are doing, you will be successful."

—ALBERT SCHWEITZER

"My number one rule in business and in life is to have fun. If you don't enjoy what you're doing, then you shouldn't be doing it. It's that simple. Life is not a dress rehearsal, so, like a child, we shouldn't waste time doing things that don't light our fires."

—RICHARD BRANSON

It started as a straightforward genetics experiment.

William Muir, a Purdue University geneticist, wanted to increase egg-laying productivity among hens. He suspected he could boost egg output by breeding the most prolific hens. After a few generations, Muir reasoned, this would result in a high-performance flock of hens.

In one cage, he placed average hens—the control group.

In another cage, he placed a test group of high achievers, the most productive hens—the Super Chickens.

He then let both groups get down to business. Several generations later, the average hens were producing more eggs than they were at the start of the experiment. These average hens were plump, feathery, and healthy. They thrived.

And those elite hens? The Super Chickens ended up killing each other. Only one-third survived, and those that remained were pecked bare. For the high achievers, it was, literally, the survival of the fittest.

Why did the average hens thrive, and the overachievers wither? Because of social dynamics and individual vs. group productivity. In an article titled "When the Strong Outbreed the Weak," William Muir and David Wilson explain:

> The reason for this perverse outcome is easy to understand, at least in retrospect. The most productive hen in each cage was the biggest bully, who achieved her productivity by suppressing the productivity of the other hens. Bullying behavior is a heritable trait, and several generations were sufficient to produce a strain of psychopaths.

Does your workplace or industry remind you of that Super Chicken environment?

When you put a bunch of talented and ambitious individuals in a defined space, chances are they will begin to peck each other bare. We see this manifest in all kinds of domains, from politics to academia—but especially in the corporate world. Competition for jobs, advancement, deals, clients, and survival is fierce. This intensity holds in Hollywood, in Silicon Valley, on Wall Street, and in most industries.

Brutal competition, internal and external, is the workplace reality for many high achievers. Accelerating technological disruption, globalization, and AI are reordering almost every industry and profession—yes, including those precious white-collar jobs. Workplace competition will only intensify, especially as the global labor market continues to flatten as companies source work-from-home knowledge employees from practically anywhere.

I do not suggest you aspire to be average. On the contrary, an enriched life goes way beyond average. I *am* proposing an awareness of the sometimes high price of workplace social dynamics. A meta-analysis study by researchers at Harvard and Stanford found work stress is just as detrimental to a person's health as secondhand cigarette smoke. There are many sources of workplace stress—long hours, job insecurity, and competitiveness in the chicken cage.

You will probably spend at least one-third of your life working, and considerably more if you are a super achiever. Professional satisfaction plays an outsized role in enriching life. You may not be able to tame your workplace environment. However, you can control how you engage in and relate to it. These seven work-hacking strategies can help you bust out of the chicken coop:

1. Take Money Out of the Equation
2. Work Fewer Hours
3. Leverage Your Strengths
4. Craft Your Job, on Your Terms
5. 'Help Me Help You'
6. Innovate Your Career Arc
7. Create Optionality

1. TAKE MONEY OUT OF THE EQUATION

Consider this job satisfaction litmus test: Do you enjoy your job so much that you would sacrifice a quarter of your salary? (Could you even afford to take a 25 percent pay cut?)

The most important career decision you can make is to take money out of the equation.

To improve job and career satisfaction, focus on the content and Impact of your work, the personal growth you gain through work, and the non-tangible benefits of your work. Do not focus on money.

Taking money out of the work equation runs counter to both instinct and conventional wisdom. They certainly don't teach this in business school. Brilliant people routinely make suboptimal career decisions based on financial factors alone. Remove money from career decisions by concentrating on:

- The longer-term opportunity
- The potential Impact the company can have on society
- The Impact and value add you can deliver to the company
- Your fit with, and ability to contribute to, the company culture

By spotlighting the opportunity rather than the reward, you stand to maximize both professional and personal satisfaction. As long as you add value, the money usually follows. Don't chase the money. Let it find you.

Here is how you can take money out of the work equation.

First, do not make career decisions based primarily on the paycheck, such as deciding to join company A over company B because of the compensation, or staying at a company *only* because the pay is good. While I am guilty of the latter (and paid dearly mentally, as a result), I have never ever taken a job because of the pay. In fact, in the few times I changed jobs, I always chose opportunities that excited me—roles in which I felt I could contribute, learn, and grow, as well as enjoy the company of the people with whom I would spend considerable time. Often, these opportunities did not pay the most upfront.

Second, once you decide on the opportunity, get paid what you deserve. Unless you contribute to a nonprofit, I do not suggest you discount your compensation. Compensation has many components: cash (salary/bonus), equity, and intangible benefits. Intangible compensators include contributing to an inspiring Mission and enjoying time flexibility. The goal is to maximize your *total compensation*, including job satisfaction and the value of your time.

Suppose you are a lawyer at a top-drawer firm, and your priority is to pursue a lifestyle balance rather than billable hours. You could take a pay cut and move to a less pressurized role that would give you more control over your time. You could choose to move to a startup and earn equity rather than the high income associated with billable hours. You could simply reduce the hours that you work. Very successful lawyers have happily taken all three approaches.

I have learned firsthand that a pay cut pays off.

While running a company as chief executive, I sought more flexibility with my time. I enjoyed the intellectual stimulation and challenge of leading a company in a highly disrupted industry. Still, I wanted to focus on family and non-professional priorities as well. I proposed a 20 percent reduction in my compensation, in exchange for 20 percent more time. This 20 percent more time equated to one day a week on top of my vacation entitlement. That amounted to just under eighty days a year! Think about it. Eighty days, plus weekends and public holidays, to do my own thing. That is a life satisfaction game-changer.

My pitch to the company was simple: the company would save money, and I would remain 100 percent accountable and responsible for the business. It was a win-win situation.

To be clear, I did not propose a pay cut because I disliked my job. I took a pay cut because I prioritized time *more*. I took a pay cut to *buy* time.

This voluntary pay cut produced one giant unanticipated consequence: I enjoyed work much more. Giving up 20 percent of my salary changed my mindset entirely. Before the salary cut, I was frustrated by the disruption ripping through my industry, and I often thought *they do not pay me enough*. I was focused on financial rewards. After surrendering one-fifth of my salary, my focus shifted back to the job content, the people, and what attracted me to the role in the first place.

It turns out my experience—though uncommon (or at least unspoken) in corporate America—is not an outlier. The *Harvard Business Review* reports:

> More than 9 out of 10 employees…are willing to trade a percentage of their lifetime earnings for greater meaning at work. Across age and salary groups, workers want meaningful work badly enough that they're willing to pay for it.

Research in 2019 by the work management platform Wrike corroborates this finding. Looking at full-time adult workers at organizations with 200 or more employees (with male and female employees equally represented), Wrike discovered:

> Over half (58 percent) of respondents have accepted a lower-paying position in the pursuit of happiness, indicating that more money doesn't buy happiness at work for the majority of people.

Diving into this phenomenon, Wrike further examined the factors contributing to workplace happiness, revealing a stark disparity between the happiness factors for unhappy employees and for happy employees. Among unhappy employees, money ranks most important:

Happiness Factors for Unhappy Employees

1. Compensation
2. Flexible hours/remote work
3. Meaningful work
4. Company culture/reputation
5. Office location
6. Management/leadership

However, among happy employees, the connection with compensation looks very different. Job content wins.

Happiness Factors for Happy Employees

1. Meaningful work
2. Flexible hours/remote work
3. Compensation
4. Management/leadership

5. Company culture/reputation
6. Office location

Still not convinced a pay cut pays off? A work-life balance survey conducted by Joblist indicates that 31 percent of workers would be willing to give up some of their income for better work-life balance. "It also appears that the higher up the corporate ladder one climbs, the more money they would be willing to sacrifice to have a better balance," the Joblist study concludes.

Taking money out of the equation, or at least downgrading its importance, shifts the focus. You pivot from extrinsic rewards (such as money and status) to intrinsic rewards, like the warm and fuzzy feeling you get from accomplishing something personally meaningful. Concentrating on job content rather than compensation translates to workplace happiness.

If you are on your way toward financial Independence or perhaps have already arrived, go ahead and take that pay cut. Enjoy the payoff.

2. WORK FEWER HOURS

In Japan, the work culture among salarymen is rigorous: follow the chain of command, spend long hours in the office, drink with colleagues after work, and take few vacations. The Japanese even have a term for "death by overwork."

Not to be outdone, in 2018, Americans worked on average one hundred more hours than the Japanese, according to OECD data. Workers in both countries typically take far fewer vacation days than they have.

We work long and hard. But does quantity translate to quality? Does more work result in more productivity?

Usually not. I can anecdotally attest that more office hours do not translate into more output—and certainly not higher quality output.

There is a galaxy of work productivity literature. The bottom line: we are not machines. There are diminishing returns to both the quantity and quality of our output after some time. The productivity paradox provides more evidence that less is often more.

"Research shows 4-day workweeks and 6-hour workdays can be just as productive. And result in happier employees," Jeff Haden writes in *Inc.* "In hindsight," he declares, "5-day workweeks and 8-hour workdays will be considered the dumbest management practices of all time." One study in the U.K. found the average office worker spends less than three productive hours in a workday. That's after factoring in coffee breaks, social media breaks, chitchat with colleagues, and other time sucks.

Our goal, of course, is much bigger than on-the-job productivity. Our goal is an enriched life. Liberating your time to target your highest priorities forms the essence of an enriched life.

How to free your time? Work fewer hours.

Cut out those time sucks. Concentrate your work energy on productive uses of your time, and unleash more hours in the day for your priorities. Fewer hours on the job does not mean fewer *quality* hours. In the office, cut the nonsense and fixate on what is most important, just as you should in your personal life.

In August 2019, Microsoft ran an experiment in Japan, the country of "death by overwork." The company implemented a four-day workweek and assessed its year-on-year change in productivity. If the entire Japanese subsidiary worked 20 percent less in August 2019 than in August 2018, you would expect productivity to decrease, right? Guess what happened? Productivity increased by 40 percent—with employees working 20 percent less.

Taking that 20 percent pay cut, I eliminated all the trivial drains of time and squeezed 100 percent of my output into 80 percent of my workdays. I stopped attending unnecessary meetings and doing activities that did not add value. My number of days in the office decreased, but my efficiency increased. From the company's point of view, my output was constant if not improved.

Much of the workplace productivity discussion revolves around the optimal number of hours of work each day or number of days to work a week. There exists another possibly transformative way to work less—the sabbatical. "Sabbatical" is often a euphemism for involuntary time off between jobs. When I refer to a sabbatical, I mean an intentional, planned, purposeful, and enriching break. The time off may be between jobs, but it doesn't have to be.

While common in academia, sabbaticals are uncommon in American business. Fewer than 25 percent of all US companies offer sabbaticals, according to *Fast Company*. For those companies that do, the threshold is typically after ten years of service.

How unfortunate. Sabbaticals are a robust way to improve work and life satisfaction. Employees benefit. So does the company, in two ways. First, the employee returns to the office recharged, with fresh ideas and often a new perspective. Second, as workers cover for each other, the office cross-pollinates. Employees better understand each other's roles and responsibilities. This integrates the office and improves teamwork.

You might think *a sabbatical would never be possible at my company. Never here.* You would be surprised. Amazon, for instance, is not the kind of company usually associated with work-life balance. Amazon is the second-largest private employer in the United States, and *The New York Times* describes its workplace as "bruising." Yet, one of Amazon's most senior executives, who heads the fast-growing entertainment and advertising businesses inside the tech conglomerate (as well as all Mergers & Acquisitions), took a year-long sabbatical in 2020. "It's never easy to find a good time for a break when always scaling so fast, but now feels like the right time for me and my family," the executive told colleagues in an internal email.

If an executive at the center of the action at one of the most valuable companies on the planet can leverage a year off work, chances are you can too.

You may think *a sabbatical is a career killer.* Not long ago, *The Wall Street Journal* profiled the head of a major insurance company, Guardian Life. At age forty-one, this executive stepped back from the prime of her career for a two-year break. Now she is CEO.

In my career, I have taken two sabbaticals while climbing the corporate ladder.

The first was during my tenure with the Hollywood studio. For some time, I itched to take a chunk of time off to do something spectacular that could not fit into a conventional vacation. During one contract negotiation, I asked for an unpaid sabbatical if I renewed my employment contract. The response I expected was a firm "NO," for the company did not have a formal sabbatical program, nor was I aware of any precedent.

I asked, anyway.

The follow-up question from my boss surprised me: "How long?"

I had anticipated many objections and questions, but not this one. I never expected the studio even to *consider* the idea. I blurted out two months, which was just long enough for me to cycle coast-to-coast across the United States if I pedaled fast enough. Two months, I also reasoned, was short enough that my absence would not inconvenience the business nor my colleagues too much. A few days later, after running this sabbatical request up the corporate flagpole, I got the response I had hoped for, but did not expect: YES! The one reasonable condition attached to this unpaid sabbatical was mutual agreement on the timing.

I learned two lessons from that experience. Sometimes you just need to ask. I also discovered that a two-month leave is way too short. I finished the two months victoriously, having cycled 3,700 miles from Oregon to New Hampshire in just fifty days. This taste of "freedom" left me wanting much, much more. I returned to the workplace environment described in chapter 1 and immediately noticed that *nothing* had changed. But I had changed. My sabbatical gave me a real-world frame of reference. I realized I, and my priorities, no longer fit my corporate role.

Before long, I was plotting how to take another, more extended sabbatical.

My second sabbatical began less than a year after my first one ended. After months of Monday Morning Malaise described in chapter 1, I finally left the Hollywood studio—and soon thereafter embarked upon my second sabbatical. I was a corporate ladder kind of guy looking for more out of life than just climbing that ladder. I embraced this nine-month sabbatical with an energy and intensity I had not experienced in *years*. That second sabbatical extended my professional life and profoundly enriched my personal life. Those irreplaceable nine months were filled with intentional family and personal adventures, including my cycling trip across Europe.

When I climbed back onto a high rung of the corporate ladder with a different employer, I felt reinvigorated, and enthused to focus on work once again. Taking that sabbatical was one of my very best career moves.

In thinking about how to accomplish more at work, many professionals instinctively add more hours to the workday and more days to the workweek. Sometimes, in the middle of a big project, a big deal, or a seasonably busy period, more *is* more. More hours are needed to get the job done. But usually, in steady-state, if you concentrate your efforts you can maintain a high-quality standard by working a little (or sometimes a lot) less.

Consider this: When you go full speed, a small reduction in the number of hours yields a disproportionate improvement in your quality of life. In some professions, an eighty-hour workweek is standard. At this pace, you may only have five or so hours of free time a week. Reducing to *only* seventy-five hours a week *doubles* your discretionary time. That makes an enticing trade.

Resist the natural temptation to add more work hours to the day. Do the opposite. Think of it not as a marathon but as a sprint—an intellectual dash with concentrated bursts of energy and firepower.

Identify what matters most at work, just as you identified your Hierarchy of Priorities in chapter 3, and attack those work priorities effectively and efficiently.

3. LEVERAGE YOUR STRENGTHS

My Hollywood career began in my final semester at Columbia Business School, when the studio recruited me for a financial analyst role. It was an entry-level MBA job to help the film company decide which motion pictures to greenlight. Facing considerable student debt, I was determined to get my foot in the door—but I was just not suited for that analyst role.

The studio flew me to LA for a round of interviews. I met first with the senior vice president of finance for one of the company's film labels. The executive looked at my resume and immediately noticed the disconnect. "You don't want this job," he told me. "Yes, I do!" I countered. Around we went, as I tried to convince a skeptical executive how suited I was for a job I did not fit. The SVP suggested another arm of the studio would be a better match. He sent me to see an executive who was not on my official interview schedule.

I eventually got a job with the studio, but in a different role and in a different part of the world than expected. That job search had a successful conclusion. I often observe, directly and indirectly, an unhappy ending when the role does not fit—perhaps due to temperament, perhaps skillset—and the executive overstretches. Overextending yourself in a position for which you just are not suited is a recipe for misery. For whatever reason, people insert themselves into industries, companies, and functional roles that they do not match. It is painful for everyone involved.

To excel at work and in life, leverage your strengths. See where you can add the most value, and deliver that value. You will be rewarded for it. More importantly, focusing on value-add fosters an enriched life. As we mentioned in chapter 2, making an Impact is one of the eight Essentials. In one study conducted by the Society for Human Resource Management, 90 percent of employees consider "contribution of work to [the] organization's business goals" to be either very important or important to job satisfaction.

Capitalizing on what you're best at is the *surest* (but not *only*) path to make an Impact in this universe.

The management guru, Peter Drucker, wrote thirty-nine business books and consulted for some of the world's biggest companies in the second half of the twentieth century. He also authored a seminal article entitled "Managing Oneself." First written in 1999 but republished since, Drucker offers enduring wisdom on the value of leveraging strengths:

> Concentrate on your strengths. Put yourself where your strengths can produce results…One should waste as little effort as possible on improving areas of low competence. It takes far more energy to improve from incompetence to mediocrity than it takes to improve from first-rate performance to excellence… Do not try to change yourself—you are unlikely to succeed. But work hard to improve the way you perform.

The positive psychologists call these signature strengths. The source of work and life satisfaction, they say, is to use as many of these talents as possible. In *Authentic Happiness*, Martin Seligman identified twenty-four signature strengths, which range from "curiosity in the world" to "self-control." These are not hard skills, like knowing how to use a spreadsheet. Signature strengths reflect deep personality characteristics—the stuff that makes you tick. Research at the University of Missouri demonstrates a high positive correlation between the use of these strengths at work and productivity, engagement, and job satisfaction.

Drucker recommended feedback analysis to discover your strengths. Whenever you make a crucial decision (such as determining goals in your Life Plan or Annual Financial Plan), write down the intended results. After some period, say a year, compare expectations to results. This feedback analysis will illuminate your talents and weaknesses.

Realistically, finding a job that unifies all of your signature strengths may be a tall order. Do not put too much burden on satisfying all of your signature strengths at work. That is a lot to expect from any job. You may need to design such a role or figure out other areas of your life where you can leverage your signature strengths.

Your strengths should be present in your life, even if they're not present in your career. Suppose you are a data scientist, and one of your signature strengths is "appreciation of beauty and excellence." You may find beauty in numbers. Alternatively, you can find a hobby that activates that strength. You will feel more positive about your career when you're deploying a key strength outside of work, as opposed to when that strength is totally absent from your life.

4. CRAFT YOUR JOB, ON YOUR TERMS

The perfect job rarely exists. You may need to customize a role to maximize job satisfaction and engagement. In the organizations I have run, we often accommodated valued executives by customizing positions. Job crafting ranges from being flexible with hours to shuffling responsibilities so that executives stay challenged and engaged. I would rather craft a job to retain an executive than fill a vacancy with an unproven executive. The inverse also applies: it is often better to tweak a role in a company that values you than to prove yourself to a new organization.

Job crafting also applies to senior positions.

Jeremy Butler (a pseudonym) is the ultimate job crafter. As an attorney, he provided legal support for some of the biggest IPOs in the past decade. After a thirty-plus-year career in negotiating, structuring, and papering mega deals, he retired at age fifty.

Overnight he went from the top of a top-drawer Wall Street law firm to retirement. "Retirement feels like the first day after school exams finish—every day," he expounds. "But after that, there comes the kind of shock, because work has been so all-encompassing. I now have to start redefining me: what I want to do and who I want to be."

To reverse years of working, he took up Pilates, yoga, and Japanese martial arts and worked to improve his golf game. It is not as easy as it sounds because close friends still work full time. After completing several personal projects, including renovating a property and traveling extensively, he started to get a career itch. He did not want to return to full-time law practice, but he did want to leverage his strengths and enjoy some professional engagement.

Butler designed an unusual arrangement with one of Wall Street's biggest and most well-known legal firms. In this uniquely crafted role, he practices law and participates in intellectually stimulating dealmaking, but on a part-time basis *on his terms*. Butler enjoys scheduling latitude without the baggage that accompanies a managing partner position.

Another real-world example: Senior HR executive, Eleanor Rimbaud, (a pseudonym) was bored with corporate work. She sought professional engagement, stimulation, and time flexibility and found all three in an industry in which she had no experience. Representing the pilots' union of a major airline, she leveraged her HR expertise to create a sweet gig with a 2.5-day workweek. Although she only worked part-time, she negotiated full benefits and vacation—which worked out to be ten weeks of leave per year. Designing this role, she landed on the optimal professional and personal balance.

Jeremy Butler and Eleanor Rimbaud aspired to professional contribution—on their terms. They designed meaningful roles in rigid industries. This job crafting provided professional satisfaction without compromising life satisfaction.

5. 'HELP ME HELP YOU'

There are a few principles to keep in mind when pursuing these career-enriching strategies. A natural hurdle is fear of the downside: *What if the company says no?*

It is the company's prerogative to say no. In many cases, you will be no worse off from having had the conversation. However, there is an enormous upside to asking the question. You may get what you want. And if you don't, you may gain clarity on how the company values you. To make this calculated decision, do the math in the Vanquish the "Fear Factor" exercise from the previous chapter.

Do not let ego ("I'm far too important and way too busy") get in the way. These are excuses for inaction. Would a change improve your work satisfaction? If so, then ask for one. That something is hard is no reason not to do it.

Position your ask from the company's point of view. Do not tell the company what's in it for you; emphasize what this does for them. Outline benefits of the proposed arrangement to the company, and ways to mitigate or eliminate the downsides (such as, guaranteeing productivity based on whatever metric you measure). In particular, emphasize how this request helps your boss. For example, you might help train colleagues. To paraphrase *Jerry Maguire*, tell your company how they can help you help them.

When I requested a two-month sabbatical, I positioned it as a quid-pro-quo to sign a new employment contract. Both sides got what they wanted. I also pointed out that the requested leave was short. Therefore, any inconvenience would be minimal, and there were internal resources to mitigate this inconvenience.

In getting the 20 percent additional time, I made this palatable to the company in two ways. First, I maintained 100 percent of my KPIs, such that the reduction in my work hours did not adversely affect the company. Second, I did not ask for something without giving anything. I volunteered a 20 percent pay cut: The company got 100 percent performance for 20 percent less cost. That is a good deal.

6. INNOVATE YOUR CAREER ARC

Most careers occupy forty or more years of prime adulthood. Dissatisfaction with this extended work-life equation has grown in recent years. One response is the Financial Independence Retire Early (FIRE) movement, which spread virally—particularly among millennials wanting to avoid their parents' work/life misery. Through extreme frugality, people took FIRE to extremes. It was common to hear about twenty-somethings retiring on modest nest eggs—known as Lean FIRE, in the vernacular. FIRE's appeal emanates from unhappiness at work, or unwillingness to dedicate the vast majority of adulthood to employment.

COVID-19 rained on many FIREs. However, the root problem has not gone away. It *is* important to innovate your career arc, especially given elongated lifespans. Your professional trajectory does not have to be a continuous multi-decade marathon. You can construct an enriching career track as a series of half marathons, or even 10k's, with plenty of recovery time in between.

Consider these alternatives to prevent work from turning into a grueling ultra-marathon:

Retire early-ish instead of early. Work a bit longer, but still retire substantially ahead of schedule. This gives you enough runway to build career capital as well as financial capital. Early-ish retirement also gives you plenty of time to do something meaningful post-career, or even develop a second career.

Adopt a portfolio career. Sometimes the best way to construct your ideal job, activate your signature strengths professionally, and enjoy time flexibility is through a portfolio career. This type of career juggles multiple part-time roles, typically anchored around one primary assignment. Consulting is a typical way to build a portfolio career that enables you to activate multiple strengths through a bespoke combination of gigs. It also gives you similar flexibility with regard to what you seek in retirement.

PISSE. This stands for Passive Income + Sabbaticals + Selective Employment. PISSE combines all these work hack strategies, punctuated by periodic sabbaticals. PISSE affords you the intellectual and social benefits of professional contribution, some earned income, and the freedom to take chunks of time off. Yes, you can PISSE on FIRE.

These innovative career trajectories enable you to bolster career capital *and* financial capital, while enriching your life.

7. CREATE OPTIONALITY

In chapter 1 we discussed the many mindsets of the Monday Morning Malaise. Often, this misery stems not from the *job position* itself but from the perceived *lack of alternatives* to the job—that familiar feeling of being "stuck." However, many viable solutions exist.

Optionality is the optimum solution. When work becomes a choice and not an obligation, it changes everything about the work itself.

Financial security anchors optionality and is the common denominator among strategies. Financial security mitigates dependence upon a paycheck and provides confidence and resources to live and work *on your terms*. That is why I dedicated three chapters to building financial security.

Consider:

> If you could do anything in the world right now, what would you do? Most importantly, would you continue doing what you currently do?

> Would you make better or different career decisions if you took money out of the equation?

> Would you be more satisfied professionally and personally if you could work less?

Would engagement improve if you activated more of your signature strengths at work, or in a hobby?

Would innovating your career trajectory energize you, inspire you?

If you answered affirmatively to any of the above questions, figure out a way to employ these tactics to enrich your life. That may mean figuring out how to accelerate financial security; fast-tracking optionality is the ultimate work- and life-hacking strategy.

Sometimes, you do not have the option to take a pay cut or sabbatical, or to remove money from the work equation. Sometimes, it is necessary to make peace with your job, even if it does not entirely satisfy. There are occasions when doing something mostly for the money for a while can accelerate longer-term financial Independence, especially if one accepts the situation with intention and with some limitations. If your situation has an endpoint and gets you closer to other important goals, then grinning and bearing it might be the best short-term solution. The decisive test should be whether the job contaminates other aspects of your life. If job unhappiness affects family and other relationships, negatively influences your outlook, or manifests in depression, anxiety, or sleeplessness, then you should not accept the status quo. Take corrective action.

ENRICH: KEY TAKEAWAYS: BUST OUT OF THE CHICKEN COOP

Professional satisfaction plays an oversized role in an enriched life. Do not settle for the Super Chicken experience. These work-hacking methods will help you bust out of the chicken coop. These strategies may appear radical. That makes them powerful. Devise a way to make these techniques work for you. Embrace them and enrich yourself, as Jeremy Butler and Eleanor Rimbaud did. In the iconic words of Mick Jagger, "You can't always get what you want, but if you try...you get what you need."

- Take money out of the work equation. Instead, concentrate on job content, Impact, personal growth, and non-tangible benefits.
- Work less. Boost productivity, not working hours. Consider ways to create more personal time, such as through a sabbatical.
- Capitalize on what you're best at.
- Design your optimal role.
- Position any request from the company's perspective—'Help me help you.'
- Innovate your professional arc; your career doesn't have to be a multi-decade ultra-marathon.
- Financial security creates optionality and that changes everything.

With these tactics to improve professional satisfaction in mind, let's take a closer look at strategies to inflate life by infusing the eight Essentials.

CHAPTER 11

HABITS FOR ENRICHED HAPPINESS

"And in the end, it's not the years in your life that count; it's the life in your years."

—ABRAHAM LINCOLN

"Action may not always bring happiness, but there is no happiness without action."

—WILLIAM JAMES, CONSIDERED THE "FATHER" OF AMERICAN PSYCHOLOGY

David Gething fashions himself as a regular guy. Married with two children, two dogs, and a cat, he runs a thriving veterinary practice that supports thousands of families and their beloved pets.

There is one more thing about Gething that you should know.

In his spare time he ran seven full marathons on seven continents in seven days, winning the first-ever World Marathon Challenge in 2015. In one week, Gething traveled more than 23,000 miles and established two world records, averaging 3:39 hours each race. He competed in Antarctica, Chile, the United States, Spain, Morocco, the United Arab Emirates, and Australia. An impressive result, especially considering he almost quit the race in Morocco.

The backstory is perhaps even more impressive.

This Aussie is not a natural sportsman. After thirteen years of "lifestyle accumulation"—eating, drinking, and merrymaking as he approached middle age—he was far from athletic. In his words, he was "overweight, unfit, unhealthy, and possibly, inside it all, unhappy." After work, he would go to the pub and enjoy food, drink, and a good night with his mates.

The turning point for Gething was when his very pregnant wife caught him sneaking a cigarette after repeated promises to quit. She asked him what kind of role model he wanted to be for their soon-to-be-born child. That vision of his future self inspired a move toward personal transformation.

In this transformation, he developed a system to blend work life, family life, and personal life into a cohesive whole to achieve big goals. Gething thinks of this as a three-way seesaw. The three planks always balance interdependently. It is not possible, he says, for all to exist equally at all times. If you push one side too far, the others will fall. The impeding factor is work. "You can work as long as you want, and then you can work some more. There comes a time when you have to say no," says Gething.

His solution? Compartmentalize family, work, and personal life, and focus intently on each at appropriate times. "It's not that the three parts are completely separate. They have to be cohesive," he tells me over iced tea.

To make time for training, which Gething views as his downtime away from work and family, he carves a disciplined schedule. He rises at 4:30 a.m., a full two hours before his kids get up. He trains hard in those two hours, but says it's not really about the fitness; it's about the uncluttered personal time. Gething returns from training by the time his kids awake at 6:30 a.m. Most nights, he returns home from work by 6:30 p.m. He disallows career and pastimes to intrude on this family time, and has maintained this schedule for years.

Workout buddies are crucial. Gething could not keep this rigorous schedule without a robust social support system. On mornings when he feels worn out, responsibility to the group gets him out of bed. Making new friends and joining social circles were part of his transformation. "It's hard when one set of friends is out at 3 a.m., and another group of friends is up at 4:30 a.m.," he observes. "You are the agglomeration of your seven closest friends. That makes me careful about who my friends are."

"I need to find something that scares me, a unique challenge. Something different and interesting," Gething explains. Every six months, he targets a big race or event somewhere in the world. These big personal goals nourish his life satisfaction. They give him focus, a reason to "get up and do it."

He always makes sure a motivating fire exists. "Secretly," he admits, "I go back to the person I was ten years ago" when he was unfit and overweight. "I always have to be a little scared, or I get lazy. At the end of 2016, I had a big triathlon race, and everyone said to take a break. Once I turned off, I fell back into the old ways."

Family trips typically combine athletic competition and family time. On a family excursion to Iceland, Gething enjoyed five days of personal time to bike around the island and run a midnight marathon, followed by seven days of family time. He blends the trips, yet separates the different spheres of life. He and his wife also make sure there is at least one family trip each year that doesn't involve any sport.

"You have to say no to things" to protect different areas of life. Take charity work. Gething spent several years doing charity work and found it rewarding and meaningful, but it does not fit in right now with the other parts of his three-way seesaw.

"It annoys me that people say being happy is successful. That is self-ish," Gething believes. "Success is not about happiness. I employ sixty people. That is sixty spouses, plus families. When you get to the point of having a good job and having everything in place, you can give back some of the inspiration. THAT is success: It is interactions and relationships."

HOW TO ESSENTIALIZE

In chapter 2 we talked about the eight Essential success factors to enrich life. These intangible elements inflate life, like air for a tire. To refresh, the eight Essentials are:

- Interpersonal connectivity
- Independence (money and time)
- Identity
- Intentionality
- Impact
- Integration
- Inspiration

❺ Invigoration

David Gething's story beautifully illustrates the enriching qualities of these Essentials. In this chapter, we'll investigate strategies to help you weave the eight Essentials into your daily routine:

1. Practice Discipline
2. Invest in the Essentials
3. Integrate
4. Add Some Happiness Boosters

All of these calibration strategies are 100 percent within your control. Individually and collectively, these four strategies will enrich your life.

1. PRACTICE DISCIPLINE

The first step to inflating life is to *take control*. Impose discipline. Technically, impose five disciplines, also known as the Five Ds.

DEMARCATE

Work-life imbalance is a modern construct. When business communication was conducted primarily through the work phone and fax, the physical boundaries between office and home ensured that even the busiest executive had some quality downtime. Thirty years ago, when you left the office, you left work. There was no round-the-clock business communication, no weekend conference calls. As digital communication and personal technology transcended physical boundaries, 24/7 communication and engagement gradually became the expectation, and now the norm.

Someone forgot to create an off button.

Then COVID-19 made things funky. On a mass scale during the pandemic lockdowns, the workplace came home. Now it's here to stay. In many companies and industries, remote working will increasingly become commonplace. We need that off button!

The solution: Impose an off button by demarcating between work and life, as David Gething does at 6:30 a.m. and 6:30 p.m. each workday. It's a judgment call where to establish those boundaries affecting evenings, weekends, and vacations. The failure to impose discipline and to demarcate will mean that work will creep into and possibly overpower every other aspect of your life.

A case in point: less than twelve hours after writing this chapter, I jumped on a conference call with a counterparty in Los Angeles. It was my Monday morning, his Sunday afternoon. I apologized for intruding on his weekend. "Oh, I have a 4 p.m. call today and a 6:30 p.m. call today, so this call fits right in! It's just another Sunday," he said.

The boundaries do not have to be absolute. You can make allowances; just be sure to set limits and honor them. For example, it is okay to glance at your work inbox on Saturday mornings. You can look at your emails when on holiday; just be sure to cap the time—ideally, no more than thirty minutes a day. (Europeans tend to switch off completely.)

Effective demarcation may mean establishing reasonable expectations with your counterparts. This involves communicating with your bosses, colleagues, and possibly with your business partners. Explain why this request for boundaries and time off is important to you. Most businesspeople will respect your wishes, especially if you agree in advance to make exceptions for urgent situations.

One immediately actionable way to demarcate *right now*: turn off email and phone alerts for new messages. Doing so reduces distraction and temptation to check messages frequently.

Effectively demarcating goes a long way to prevent the unimportant from displacing the important.

DISCERN

Prioritization involves "de-prioritization"—you decide what is necessary, and eliminate what does not make the cut. How and with whom we spend our time significantly affects life satisfaction. Our choices matter, as discussed in chapter 3. A good question to ask after any activity or interaction: *How did that experience make me feel? Do I feel energized? Or drained?*

Discernment means NO is sometimes the right response. Occasionally, it is necessary to cut people from your life and drop unimportant tasks, responsibilities, and social events. You can optimize your time by discerning how a person or activity makes you feel afterward. Identify the events and people that leach your energy and spirit.

When David Gething transformed his lifestyle from going to bed at 3 a.m. to getting up at 4 a.m. for training, he discerned by cultivating a new social circle to support his new lifestyle.

DELEGATE

Maximize the things that produce enjoyment and minimize or eliminate the things that deflate, both at home and work, if possible. Buy back your time. Delegating unpleasant and mechanical tasks ensures that your valuable time goes to the best use.

Say you'd rather spend the weekend relaxing than doing house-work or yard work. Outsource it. Is preparing dinner the last thing you want to do after a day in the office? Outsource it. In the gig economy, it is possible to find alternatives to doing most house-hold activities. Outsourcing the functions that deliver no joy can liberate you. By delegating, you will not only respect the value of your time but also Harness Time to your full benefit.

In a collaborative article titled "Buying time promotes happiness," researchers from several elite institutions looked at sample popu-lations in North America and Western Europe. "Individuals who spend money on time-saving services report greater life satis-faction," conclude the authors. "Using money to buy time can protect people from the detrimental effects of time pressure on life satisfaction."

At work, many executives hesitate to delegate due to self-preservation. This widespread concern cuts across all levels of an organization. Executives worry about losing control or delegating themselves out of a job. I take the opposite view. Delegation is good management practice; it strengthens the team and enables you to focus on areas in which you can add the most value.

Gething's business runs seven days a week. Still, to maintain boundaries, he delegates some business responsibilities so that he can consistently honor his daily 6:30 p.m. family commitment.

DAILY DOWNTIME

What ensures sustained high-level performance? Recovery. Elite athletes understand that during intense activity, muscle tissues break down. Athletes need recovery time to repair and strengthen muscles. Professionals require the same kind of restorative downtime to let the body repair itself, and to prevent burnout. Many executives understand and agree with this concept intellectually. In practice, however, they skimp on their own downtime.

The solution? Treat weekends like a vacation. Cassie Mogilner Holmes and research colleagues conducted several experiments and found that individuals who prioritize vacations are significantly happier, with more life satisfaction and positive emotion, and less negative emotion. Executives who treat the weekend as vacation are consistently happier than those who spend the weekend like the workweek. This finding holds, even for those who don't spend additional money or travel on their weekends.

David Gething makes sure to protect his weekends and to allocate some time each day to do his own thing.

In addition to making downtime for an activity that jazzes you, ensure you have that most precious form of downtime—sleep. Adequate sleep regulates quality of life and quality of work. Jeff Bezos, the Amazon CEO, prioritizes eight hours of sleep a night. In an interview with *Thrive Global*, he explains:

> If you shortchange your sleep, you might get a couple of extra "productive" hours, but that productivity might be an illusion. When you're talking about decisions and interactions, quality is usually more important than quantity.

Inadequate sleep (for most adults, less than seven hours a night) associates with a whole bunch of life- and health-reducing qualities, from increased rates of obesity, heart disease, stroke, and lower sperm count.

Sleep more and enrich your life.

DETOX

What's an antidote to a fast-paced life? Unplug. There are creative strategies to detox from tech and from stressful environments. The notion of a Tech Shabbat or twenty-four-hour hiatus from electronic screens grows in popularity. The Time Well Spent movement further advocates reigning in technology to preclude smartphone addiction.

Diet detoxes cleanse the body. Nature detoxes purify the spirit. The Outdoor Industry Association reports that fewer than 20 percent of Americans spend time outdoors more than once a week. To correct this, a burgeoning effort by Park RX America—a nonprofit dedicated to encouraging healthcare professionals to prescribe nature—gets doctors to prescribe that patients spend more time outdoors. How much time? At least two hours each week. A 2019 British study found health and well-being improve with time in nature. A word exists for this: *biophilia*, the idea that humans are happier when surrounded by nature.

David Gething regularly detoxes by surrounding himself in nature during his training and athletic competitions and makes it a point to live in a peaceful and natural environment away from the hustle and bustle of the city.

2. INVEST IN THE ESSENTIALS

Time-deficient professionals often sacrifice the Essentials in favor of seemingly more urgent, but not necessarily more important, matters. Historical data from the American Time Use Survey, compiled by the Bureau of Labor Statistics, highlights this negative trend line. Over the past decade, Americans worked longer and spent less time socializing, participating in sports and exercise, and attending community events. In short, Americans increasingly shortchange the Essentials.

The Essentials most often sacrificed have oversized importance on physical and emotional well-being, satisfaction, and happiness. These oft-compromised Essentials include Interpersonal Connectivity, Invigoration, and Inspiration.

INTERPERSONAL CONNECTIVITY

As discussed in chapter 2, in the long run, friendships and family matter most to life satisfaction, even more than wealth and professional success, according to the most extensive longitudinal study ever on this subject—and according to the most iconic investor of our time.

Warren Buffett boils success down to this:

> When you get to be my age, you'll really measure your success in life by how many of the people you want to have love you actually do love you. That's the ultimate test of how you lived your life. The more you give love away, the more you get.

This sage advice comes from a man with a $79 billion fortune. Oh, the irony: the most valuable Essential is the one you cannot buy.

Building and maintaining friendships poses a big obstacle for professionals. Explains Ken Jacquin, an executive who lives in Park City, Utah and works in Salt Lake City:

> Growing up on the East Coast, my father had a bowling night, a tennis night, and was always doing stuff with other people, often from the neighborhood…A lot of things we do to create financial success, and some success trappings, minimizes community. For example, when people get to a certain status, they like to buy a big house with a big yard and put a fence around it. The American dream. But that dream can isolate.

Connecting with people you care about, and who hopefully care about you, is the best investment you can make. Friends you can call at 3 a.m. are priceless.

Building and maintaining community takes intentional effort. If you find that making time for valued people in your life is a challenge, plan. Schedule a time and honor it just as you would a business commitment or a dentist appointment. If time or distance are barriers, go virtual. Drinks, meals, or even late-night video chats are not only possible but also increasingly popular. You can make it a party with video chat platforms like Zoom or Houseparty. The COVID-19 lockdowns have popularized virtual happy hours, dance parties, and family celebrations.

Consider building at least three social circles based on your interests. These communities might be work-related, school-related, sports-related, faith-related, or revolve around a shared affinity. The diversification of these communities provide strong support during life events such as changes in jobs and divorces.

Sometimes we need to invent communities. After Ken Jacquin moved to Park City, he had difficulty meeting like-minded friends, who often worked elsewhere. So, he started a men's book club. At the first meeting, which took place in a bar, they read *Green Eggs and Ham*. The club has since branched out beyond Dr. Seuss and the bar, with outdoor bonding activities such as go-karting.

Sometimes it takes creativity to find and connect with your tribe.

INVIGORATION

David Gething exudes Invigoration. He transformed from the bloke at the pub into an endurance athlete. This physical transformation totally invigorated his life. Exercise works like a magic pill. The Mayo Clinic cites seven compelling benefits of regular physical activity:

1. Controls weight
2. Combats health conditions and diseases
3. Improves mood
4. Boosts energy
5. Promotes better sleep
6. Puts the spark back into your sex life
7. Can be fun and social

Heck, exercise may be the pivotal puzzle piece of an enriched life! Plus, it is free.

Ten minutes of vigorous exercise is all that it takes, according to a 2016 McMaster University study. Among sedentary men, the Canadian kinesiologists found that ten minutes of intense interval exercise improved cardiometabolic health as much as fifty minutes of moderate continuous exercise—"despite a fivefold lower exercise volume and time commitment." Yet, according to the Centers for Disease Control, less than a quarter of American adults meet the aerobic and muscle-strengthening guidelines for physical activity.

Put exercise in the calendar as an inviolate commitment. Schedule and treat fitness as you would any important responsibility. Make it routine (i.e., integrate it!) and figure out a way to make it fun. Exercise can be social, as it is for David Gething, or you can put money on the line with a trainer or a class. Wondering where to start? Consider the Seven-Minute Workout, which you can do anywhere. Google it.

In the context of an elongated or even one hundred-year life, this vitality is vital.

INSPIRATION

A regular source of frustration among professionals is the absence of intellectual stimulation. This happens when we become highly proficient in a specialized skill. It also happens at work when we disengage from, or just get bored with, our jobs. It also often occurs when we leave the workforce. If inspiration does not organically exist in your life, find it. Or create it. Don't accept its absence.

When did you last try or learn something completely new? Anyone who has spent more than ten seconds with a toddler understands his or her fixation on "Why?" Our biology embeds curiosity. We are wired to ask questions. When we actively pursue new information, the brain releases the feel-good hormone dopamine, which creates a positive feedback loop. As we age, we stop asking so many questions. We lose curiosity. We often do not permit ourselves as adults to explore innate interests, like we did as kids.

Each of us has a natural comfort zone—that space where minimal risk and stress exist. Relative comfort produces steady performance. But to maximize performance, we need some anxiety—"Optimal Anxiety," as psychologists call it. Optimal Anxiety lies just beyond our comfort zone. The magic happens in this Discomfort Zone. That is where we challenge ourselves. We are more productive, creative, engaged, and energized, and we perform and live to our potential.

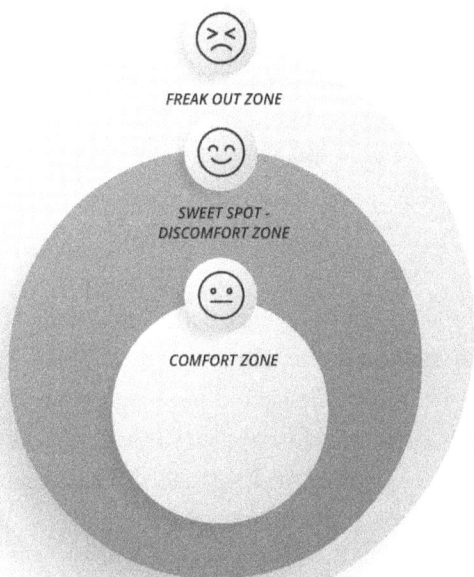

FREAK OUT ZONE

SWEET SPOT - DISCOMFORT ZONE

COMFORT ZONE

For inspiration, indulge your curiosity and steer toward your Discomfort Zone. There's also a life-enriching fringe benefit to inquisitive thinking: better relationships.

Curious people tend to have more and better Interpersonal Connectivity. George Mason University's Todd Kashdan has researched the interplay between curiosity and social relationships. His research finds that curiosity promotes intimacy in social conversations, conflict resolution, and even enhances romantic relationships. "You may not be able to change your happiness by turning a dial," Keshan tells U.C. Berkeley's *Greater Good Magazine*," but you can change your curious mindset—you can make yourself more curious—in the moment, and that will make a big difference in your life."

3. INTEGRATE

TARGET COHESION, NOT BALANCE

Trying to maintain a delicate and exact work-life equilibrium is not easy. Even if you momentarily find balance, it is mighty hard to sustain. "If work-life balance were a solvable problem," quips Charles Scott from chapter 3, "the ancient Greeks would have figured it out."

Rather than target work-life balance in 50-50 binary terms, which requires constant perfection, change the formula: Fuse the spheres of your life into a cohesive and complete whole. Integrate the personal, professional, and financial so that everything fits together and accommodates all the Essentials. A Venn diagram depicts this fusion with you at the center:

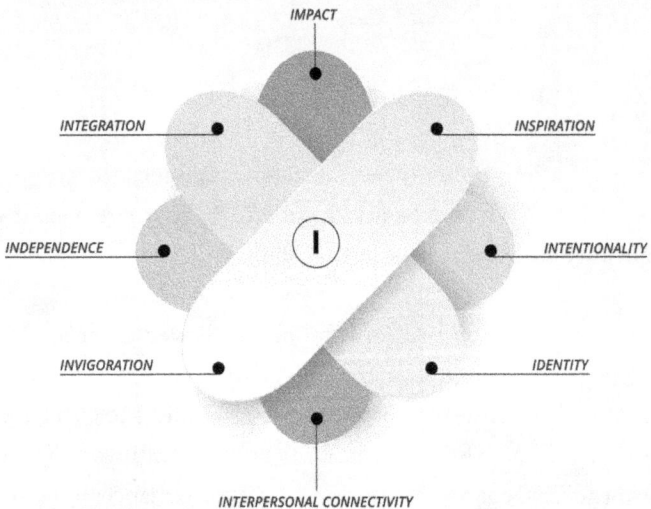

Integration occurs when your responsibilities, activities, and interests "peacefully coexist," to borrow David Gething's phrase. The more we integrate our interests, obligations, and priorities, the more grounded and in control we feel. We accommodate everything important. As we learned from Airin Zainul in chapter 9, the more we integrate a major goal into our lives, the more likely we will stick with and accomplish it.

Multipurposing is a practical way to integrate Essentials into daily routines. Many regard commuting, for example, as a negative aspect of modern professional life. How might you neutralize, or perhaps even convert it into a positive, commuting experience? Maybe you can ride a bike instead of driving. If you choose to drive, call friends during your evening commute. Listen to audiobooks or podcasts to stretch your mind and indulge your curiosity. These quick actionable tactics enable you to convert a mundane daily ritual into an enriching activity by adding Invigoration, Interpersonal Connectivity, and Inspiration.

APPRECIATE THE WHOLE, NOT THE HOLES

Integration is larger than just fitting everything together. Integration also acknowledges and appreciates the big picture of your life—what you *have*. This contrasts with a materialistic mindset that obsesses about what you *don't have*. To integrate, acknowledge, and appreciate the whole, not the holes. This is where gratitude and giving back come in. They are salient features of Integration.

There are several ways to fuse gratitude into your day: maintaining a gratitude journal, telling others you are thankful, or that old-fashioned technique, saying Grace before a meal. Expressing gratefulness bestows a host of physical and psychological benefits. Research by Robert A. Emmons, the author of *Thanks!: How The New Science of Gratitude Can Make You Happier*, suggests that expressing gratitude can increase happiness by 25 percent.

Giving is a form of appreciation. Giving makes us happier. Elizabeth Dunn and Michael Norton looked at different ways of spending money in *Happy Money: The Science of Happier Spending*. They found that spending money on other people, regardless of the amount, makes us happier than spending money on ourselves. They examined this phenomenon across different cultures and found the same magnitude of happiness increase.

4. ADD SOME HAPPINESS BOOSTERS

David Gething's story demonstrates two other noteworthy contributors to enrichment: a focus on experiences, and always having something to look forward to. These happiness boosters go hand in hand.

SHARED EXPERIENCES

The joys from toys do not last long. Just watch any kid playing with discarded boxes a few hours after unwrapping presents on Christmas morning. That is hedonic adaptation, our tendency to return to a stable level of happiness after a positive or negative event. Take getting a raise. There is a short-term boost from receiving a higher salary, but the happiness increase fizzles over time. For long lasting and meaningful satisfaction, research shows experiences are most consistent sources of joy, especially when shared with the people who mean the most to us.

ANTICIPATION

By taking family vacations at least three times a year, David Gething creates shared experiences. These vacations also serve another useful purpose, which further boosts satisfaction levels: they give him something to look forward to. Anticipation contributes to happiness in a big way. That's why the forward-looking Life Plan is such a valuable tool. Having something big, challenging, and aspirational to anticipate fosters focus and purpose, improves motivation, and helps keep you moving forward.

VACATIONS

If exercise is a magic pill, then a proper and well-planned vacation is the elixir. You will get it all on an enjoyable holiday: downtime, detox, connectivity, Invigoration, Inspiration, and the chance to restore and rejuvenate. Experiencing a new place and leaving your comfort zone stimulates your senses and multiplies the benefits of the vacation. As a MasterCard ad might say: the cost of a vacay is one thing, but a good vacation is priceless.

Despite all the great things going for holidays, many time-deficient professionals do not take advantage of this elixir. *Travel + Leisure* magazine estimates US workers left 662 million vacation days unused in 2018. This wasn't always the case. Around the year 2000, Americans started working longer hours and taking fewer vacations. (In the good old days, circa 1970, Americans took more holidays than the French, who are world-class experts at taking time off.) Moreover, even when we do go on vacation, we have a hard time unplugging. A 2017 Harris poll found that two-thirds of Americans report working during holidays.

To solve this, treat your vacation like the old-fashioned break your grandparents used to enjoy. Plan. Unite family or friends for mind-blowing shared experiences. Then demarcate like crazy to defend the integrity of your vacation, as you would any important obligation.

David Gething multipurposes his vacations: he combines a holiday with sports and with family, often in a different part of the world.

He indulges curiosity by planning these experiences in exotic destinations and organizes well in advance to build anticipation.

UNSCHEDULED, UNSTRUCTURED TIME

Children require playtime to develop. Adults need the same. The Italian word for happiness is *dolce far niente* or "sweet doing nothing." Laurie Santos teaches "Psychology and the Good Life" (the most popular course in Yale's history) and hosts *The Happiness Lab* podcast. Santos explains in *Afar* magazine:

> There are studies showing that people who have unscheduled time, and who commit to unscheduled time, tend to be happier overall than people who don't. Overly scheduled time can make us feel anxious...There's also research suggesting that when we have more open time, we tend to be more social.

ENRICH: KEY TAKEAWAYS: HABITS FOR ENRICHED HAPPINESS

While on vacation in Bali, I spotted this sign:

HAPPINESS IS NOT A DESTINATION. IT'S A WAY OF LIFE.

We create happiness by intentionally self-calibrating. David Gething transformed into a world-class record-setting athlete while nurturing a family and a thriving business. Gething practices the Five Ds fully. He effectively demarcates, discerns social relationships, delegates responsibilities at work, faithfully enjoys daily downtime, and detoxes in nature. Gething also adds plenty of happiness boosters. He prioritizes shared experiences and plans family vacations far in advance to keep looking forward. His story illustrates the enriching effect of integrating the eight Essentials into your life.

As a takeaway, here are two short and Impactful exercises. The first exercise, "Magic Hour," gets you thinking about what life satisfaction may mean to you and what an enriched life could look like. The second exercise, "Add What's Missing," will get you thinking about how to integrate the Essentials into your life one step at a time.

To Self-Calibrate:

- Impose discipline with the Five Ds—Demarcate, Discern, Delegate, Daily Downtime, Detox.
- Invest in the Essentials—Interpersonal Connectivity, Invigoration, Inspiration.
- Get into your Discomfort Zone.
- Integrate the eight Essentials for cohesion and completeness.
- Add happiness boosters—shared experiences, anticipation, holidays, unstructured time.

ENRICH: TAKE ACTION: THE MAGIC HOUR

1. Imagine you have a twenty-five-hour day. While the rest of the world revolves around a twenty-four-hour cycle, you have the gift of time: an extra hour each day. Now consider:

How would you spend this extra hour?

Why?

Would this hour materially improve your life?

2. If this magic hour would improve your life, how can you perform some magic with your schedule to actualize it? What can you do to reprioritize or rearrange your schedule to incorporate this twenty-fifth-hour activity into your twenty-four-hour day?

ENRICH: TAKE ACTION: ADD WHAT'S MISSING

The eight Essentials enrich life and inflate satisfaction. Over time, their absence depletes vitality.

1. Take a personal Essentials inventory using the question prompts in chapter 2.

2. Which of the Essentials would you like more of in your life? Would this increased presence yield a definite increase in your satisfaction level?

3. Practically, how might you increase the presence of the missing or deficient element(s)? What habits can you adopt that will infuse the Essential(s) into your life? Do the Five Ds, multitasking, or cutting something that yields no positive benefit, offer a solution?

HARNESS TIME

Are you Time promiscuous? Is that a good thing?

How to get over the "I'm too busy" hurdle?

What can we possibly learn about Time from the COVID-19 pandemic?

Cassie Mogilner, an associate professor at UCLA's business school, devoted a decade of research to the relationship between happiness and time. In a 2019 paper titled *It's Time for Happiness*, she advises people to:

- Focus on time (not money)
- Have neither too little nor too much time
- Spend the time they have **deliberately** (emphasis mine)

Harnessing Time is the final ENRICH step. You control your life when you control your Time.

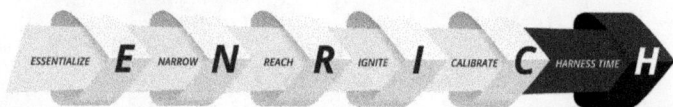

ESSENTIALIZE **E** NARROW **N** REACH **R** IGNITE **I** CALIBRATE **C** HARNESS TIME **H**

Chapter 12 explores six principles to create Time wealth. This is the last step of the ENRICH methodology: the final key to unlocking a richer, fuller life. Chapter 13 walks you through everything we have learned in this book and shows you how Alex Strah put these principles into practice to transform a potential catastrophe into an opportunity.

Plus, there's a bonus chapter. We'll examine some of the common obstacles people face when it comes to enriching, and how you can overcome them.

CHAPTER 12

— — —

IT'S ABOUT TIME

"The trouble is, you think you have time."

—Buddha

"Dream as if you will live forever. Live as if you will die tomorrow."

—Social media meme

An experience I had more than thirty years ago radically altered my relationship with Time.

My mother passed away when I was in eleventh grade.

I have few childhood memories of her being well. In and out of hospitals, she suffered numerous complications from juvenile-onset diabetes, including blindness. My school year memories involve an unending series of emergency room visits, medical procedures, and doctors.

Given this skewed sense of normalcy, the day my mother died was part of a typical weekend in February. Mom was at home. She did not feel great and spent her days in bed. That was her normal.

Our normal. She was no better nor worse off than any previous weekend. Thankfully, she wasn't in the hospital.

Throughout that weekend, I had the nagging sense to spend Time with her. Spending Time together usually meant sitting by her bed and talking or reading to her. That nagging feeling to spend more Time with my mother weighed on my conscience then, as it weighs on my conscience now.

Throughout that weekend, I also had a nagging feeling about an English poetry paper due on Monday morning. I dreaded that paper. I hated that paper, and I hated poetry. All weekend that looming deadline paralyzed and tormented me.

I recall having a distinct binary choice about *how* to spend my Time. Be with my mother or anguish over an English lit assignment about a poet whose name I cannot recall today.

The English paper won. I prioritized an English paper—a fucking high school English paper—over my mother.

I did not sense any urgency in making this conscious choice. I thought she had more Time. I thought we had more Time.

My mother passed away peacefully that Sunday evening.

Fast-forward two decades.

My beloved aunt and uncle from Tennessee visit me. We spend a great weekend together, full of fun and laughter, and share crazy experiences. I vividly recall a festive Sunday night Italian dinner. As we finish our meal and head back to my apartment, my mind shifts to Monday morning. I tense with anxiety. That was a natural cycle for me on Sunday evenings. My professional normal.

Returning to my apartment, I retreat to my study to prepare for the coming workweek. (I do not recall what I was working on, but it seemed important at that moment.)

My perceptive uncle notices my change in demeanor and senses my anxiety. He enters my study to share some of his considerable wisdom. I politely invite him in, but work issues preoccupy my thoughts.

"Time accelerates," he proceeds to tell me with enough of a Southern drawl that the words linger in the air. "You think you understand this," and then he pauses for what seems like an hour, with his brown eyes fixed on mine. "But you don't."

I heard my Uncle Bill that Sunday evening. It took me years to understand what he was saying.

"UNWILLINGNESS TO POSTPONE"

In one of history's most famous speeches, in 1962, fourteen months before his assassination, John F. Kennedy proclaimed his intent to put a man on the moon by the end of the decade. He described the challenge as "one we are willing to accept, one we are unwilling to postpone."

Time contradicts. Life is short. But also long. Time is a commodity; it is free and abundant, but it's also priceless and scarce. It is the confounding variable in life: we do not know how much total Time we have.

That means we must think and act both long term and short term. Living an enriched life means playing the long game and preparing to enjoy your one hundredth birthday. An enriched life also invokes urgency, an unwillingness to postpone what is most important—an unwillingness to tolerate Monday Morning Malaise.

"I don't like to waste time," says Annabelle Bond from chapter 4, who climbed the Seven Summits faster than any other woman in history. "Those who have accomplished many things in life have done it by being respectful of time."

How we think about Time markedly influences our behavior. Princeton social psychologists, John Darley and Dan Batson, conducted an experiment. They invited forty seminary students to attend a sermon about the Good Samaritan. The students individually made their way to the talk at the Princeton Theological Seminary. Each student received one of three messages, which I paraphrase:

- You're running late
- You're on time but need to go now so you won't be late
- You have ample time and shouldn't have to wait long when you get there

The researchers hired an actor pretending to be in severe pain, situated near the entrance of the seminary. Remember, these students are preparing to be religious leaders, and they are on their way to a talk about doing good deeds.

Can you guess what happened?

Just 10 percent of the group in a hurry stopped to help; one student stepped over the man in pain. In contrast, 45 percent of the on-time students and more than 60 percent of the ample-time cohorts stopped to help.

This 1973 study highlights how the perception of Time alters attitudes and actions. Five decades later, global lockdowns to contain the coronavirus pandemic have created an unprecedented and unscripted social experiment that has at least temporarily redefined our relationship with Time.

The impact of the coronavirus—the losses of life, health, wealth, employment, and mobility—is awful. We have already lost much during this crisis, and the certainty of uncertainty filled the void. The world has collectively hit the pause button. Shelter-at-home requirements upend routines and lifestyles. Life has been simplified—as did our perceptions of Time. Suddenly, busy people have plenty of Time. Sure, there was some Netflix bingeing at first. But, consider how some behaviors have positively changed:

- Increased bonding with family and friends, virtually if not physically
- Increased sense of purpose and meaning
- Increased compassion and charitableness
- Increased appreciation for the basics, like toilet paper
- Increased capacity for family, cooking, exercise, inspiration, and passion projects
- Increased recognition of how much we need each other
- Increased respect for financial security and financial planning

The dark days of the pandemic have shed light on something extraordinary: an acute appreciation about what, fundamentally, *is* most important. "I feel for humanity if we learn nothing from all this," a friend writes to me during the early dark days of the crisis. Concludes Trish Hall in *The New York Times*: "It's too soon to know how the definition of a good life will change, but it's hard to believe that it won't."

An enriched life recognizes, values, and harnesses Time. Time is much more valuable than money. You can earn more money, but you cannot create more Time. Contemporary culture often prioritizes financial wealth over Time wealth. But isn't the best measure of wealth and success the ability to spend Time with the people and on the projects that fire you up?

THE REALITY CHECK

How we spend our Time correlates with general happiness. The 2019 World Happiness Report notes a slow ongoing decline in happiness levels in the United States since 2010. "Americans are less happy due to fundamental shifts in how they spend their leisure time," states the report, which ranks countries and cities by "how happy their citizens perceive themselves to be" using Gallup world poll data.

In the 2020 World Happiness Report, the United States ranks eighteenth among 156 countries, just ahead of the Czech Republic. Finland, for three years in a row, ranks number one in happiness. Exploring the reasons why, Catherine A. Sanderson in *Psychology Today* asserts: "the Finns understand and prioritize time over money, and undoubtedly experience greater happiness as a result."

Let's get granular.

A few years ago, MSN published some surprising facts about how we spend our Time, aggregated from various studies. In the course of an average lifespan of seventy-five years, we might spend:

Twenty-six years sleeping, and another seven years lying awake

Eleven years watching TV

Eight years shopping

Five years surfing the internet

Three years washing clothes

Two years in meetings

Men will spend eleven months staring at women (that's forty-three minutes *a day*), says the MSN report.

According to the American Time Use Survey, compiled by the Bureau of Labor Statistics, the average day for an employed American looks like this:

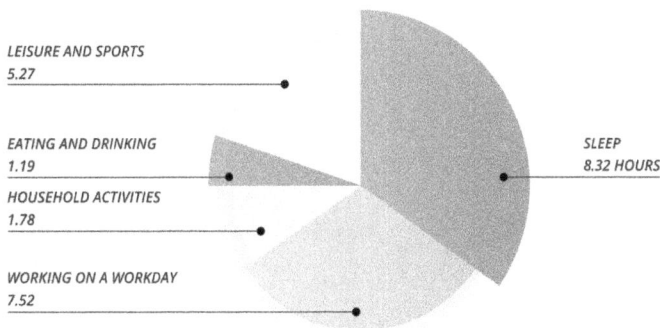

LEISURE AND SPORTS
5.27

EATING AND DRINKING
1.19

HOUSEHOLD ACTIVITIES
1.78

WORKING ON A WORKDAY
7.52

SLEEP
8.32 HOURS

This seems balanced and healthy, right? If we spend more than five hours a day on leisure and sports, why are we so unhappy? Could it be that we make the wrong choices in how we spend our Time?

If you measure the total Time we spend in front of our screens, at work and home, it adds up to more than eleven hours a day. If you are a teen or tween, that number jumps significantly higher. Our total screen Time continues to increase. In the past four years, we added about ninety minutes of screen Time to our day, according to Nielsen.

The Global Web Index calculates that we spend 142 minutes every day consumed by Facebook likes, Instagram posts, Tweets, and other social media. A Rand Corporation report probing why Americans do not exercise more had the same conclusion. Americans, the report stated, have more free Time than generally recognized and spend most of it "looking at screens (televisions, phones, or other devices)."

Think about it. One hundred forty-two minutes a day translates to more than thirty-five days a year on social media. At this rate, in the next ten years, *one full year* will be devoted to non-stop social media activity.

The data is clear: In our relationship with Time, we are promiscuous.

Perhaps it is time to reconsider that casual relationship. Perhaps it is time to commit to Time.

CREATING TIME WEALTH

If you take away one concept from this book, I hope it is this:

> **When you control your Time, you control your life. Liberate your Time from the things that do not matter, and spend your Time on what matters most.**

To create Time wealth:

1. Pivot to Abundance
2. Be Unwilling to Postpone
3. Prioritize Your Time Expenditures
4. Simulate Urgency
5. Mind the Opportunity Costs
6. Avoid Time Creep

1. PIVOT TO ABUNDANCE

We usually think about Time in terms of scarcity. So often we complain, "there are not enough hours in the day to get everything done! I'm so friggin' busy!" This way of thinking and behaving reflects Time poverty. It is the default mindset for most professionals.

Pivot that mindset. Rather than think about how *little* Time you have, consider the *abundance* of Time you have going forward. Consider all the hours and days that you can fill with purposeful activity. If you sleep seven hours each night, that leaves seventeen hours *each day*, 119 hours *each week*, and 6,188 hours *each year* to accomplish your goals!

This abundance mindset inspires, empowers, and provides a damned good reason to get out of bed each morning. With all this future Time, wallow in the pleasure of possibility. Go wild.

2. BE UNWILLING TO POSTPONE

Act now upon the things that arouse your spirit. Resist postponing what is most important to some uncertain future date. Take one of those big, audacious goals from your Life Plan, incrementalize it, and Ignite. It is that simple and that empowering. If you do not have a Life Plan yet, now is a great Time to create one.

3. PRIORITIZE YOUR TIME EXPENDITURES

Dwight Eisenhower once gave advice, now known as the Eisenhower Matrix, to some Northwestern University students. "I have two kinds of problems," Eisenhower told the students. "The urgent and the important. The urgent are not important, and the important are never urgent."

How you spend your days equates with how you spend your life. Each day, give preference first to your priorities. Then, allocate whatever Time remains to all the things which would otherwise fill up a calendar. Usually, for Time-poor professionals, it is the other way around: schedules clutter, often with urgent but inconsequential matters. This crowds out the far more important items. You can exhaust yourself responding to other people's priorities, or you can impose discipline and protect *your* priorities.

Parkinson's Law states that work, and all the other demands on your Time, expand to fill every available second. Cut out all the little BS Time sucks that drain your energy and do not enrich your life. All the *unconscious* ways we kill Time each day add up, which is why if we value Time, we must *consciously* choose how to spend it.

4. SIMULATE URGENCY

We should not allow seemingly "urgent" matters to distract. However, there is value in *simulating* urgency. When we think we have all the time in the world, we take all the time in the world. Human nature is to defer and delay. Insert yourself into your Discomfort Zone. We operate at our best when optimal anxiety exists—some pressure, some deadline to force concentrated, deliberate effort. When you add an element of Time pressure, real or artificial, it results in a positive urgency to get moving and get things done.

5. MIND THE OPPORTUNITY COSTS

What is the price of enduring Monday Morning Malaise? Or hustling to finance a lifestyle you can't afford? What else could you accomplish? What other possibilities might exist, if you did not expend your Time and energy on low priority activities? To assess the total cost of your Time usage, factor what you sacrifice by not directing your Time toward meaningful and beneficial activity.

6. AVOID TIME CREEP

Finally, to harness Time, avoid Time creep.

Can you recall in any detail the events of a random recent year of your life? A random day three weeks ago? Unless those randomly chosen moments involved some kind of significant event, chances are the days and years blend into unremarkable sameness. That is Time creep.

Time creep reflects the unconscious accumulation of Time.

Make your Time memorable by making it meaningful. A simple and highly effective way to avoid Time creep: fill your days with intentional activity, as Danny Burke from chapter 2 does. After he fell on a pile of pistachios and realized he wasn't in a plastic hell for eternity, Burke developed an acute appreciation of Time. He refuses to squander his second lease on life.

In Mary Oliver's potent words:

Instructions for living a life:

Pay Attention.

Be Astonished.

Tell About It.

ENRICH: KEY TAKEAWAYS: IT'S ABOUT TIME

It took me years to understand what my uncle meant when he told me, "Time accelerates." Our sense of Time speeds up as we age. That part is evident. But my uncle was trying to tell me something deeper. We behave as if we have infinite Time. Our choices and behaviors would be very different if we recognized reality—the finite, fleeting, ephemeral nature of Time.

Think about the common expression, "Make Time." Making Time means just that: relentless, deliberate, directed effort to create Time for yourself. Make Time for what matters. "Don't sweat the petty things," George Carlin once advised, and "don't pet the sweaty things."

Are you prepared to commit to Time?

Creating Time wealth and intentionally spending this wealth invokes all the principles of ENRICH. It also ensures you make Time for ENRICH.

- How we think about Time influences our choices and behaviors.
- How we spend Time correlates with happiness; spend your Time doing what matters most.

- Six techniques create Time wealth: think abundantly, don't defer, spend on priorities, simulate urgency, mind opportunity costs, and avoid Time creep.
- When you control your Time, you control your life.

The next chapter details a case study that puts these life optimization principles into practice.

ENRICH: TAKE ACTION: THE TIME AUDIT

1. Reflex response: Do you consider yourself Time rich or Time poor?

2. Your calendar reveals how you value Time. Take a moment to review your schedule for the past week. What fills the calendar? Do the majority of your commitments support your top priorities? Do nuisance commitments crowd out priorities? Are there some "urgent" issues? If so, are these so-called urgent issues really urgent, or for that matter, even necessary?

3. How might you rebalance your schedule? What should or could you subtract from your obligations?

4. What strategies can you put into place to harness Time? How might you simulate urgency, prioritize your Time usage and avoid Time creep, among other tactics identified in this chapter? How will you deal with the so-called "urgent" matters? You may also want to review the habits for happiness discussed in chapter 11. Be concrete. Be realistic.

5. Are you prepared to commit to Time?

CHAPTER 13

HOW TO MAKE LIFE DELICIOUS

"Wealth is the ability to fully experience life."
—Henry David Thoreau

"Tell me, what is it you plan to do with your one wild and precious life?"
—Mary Oliver

In the preceding pages, we have progressed from theory to goal setting to planning to doing. We have explored dozens of tactics to savor life. ENRICH distills these methods into six core strategies. Collectively, these strategies help you liberate your time, create financial security, and build the life you want.

ESSENTIALIZE **E** NARROW **N** REACH **R** IGNITE **I** CALIBRATE **C** HARNESS TIME **H**

These actionable strategies are time- and stress-tested, proven, and potent. Edit, shape, and personalize these tactics. Try them. Commit to the ones that fit.

When fully embraced, ENRICH transforms. Later in this chapter, we'll look at how Alex Strah used these precise methods to recast his life. Before that, however, let's recap what we've learned. An adult heart beats 115,200 times a day; these beats *enable* life. To *enrich* life:

> **Essentialize.** Eight Essentials make life delicious. Appropriately, these Essentials all start with the letter "I"—reinforcing their importance to your sense of self. Interpersonal connectivity, Independence, Identity, Intentionality, Impact, Integration, Inspiration, and Invigoration vitally contribute to your life quality. Think of individuals like Danny Burke who embrace the Essentials after a near death experience. Burke fully enjoys life with determination, energy, and intention.

> **Avoid the default setting.** If you do not set your priorities, someone else will. Take the long view to formulate your Mission Statement and Hierarchy of Priorities and to identify what matters most. Remember to first take care of your priorities, action the nonnegotiables, and make peace with your decisions. We learned this from Charles Scott in chapter 3 who enriched his life by jettisoning a corporate career.

> **Live intentionally.** Enrichment does not happen accidentally. It requires setting compelling goals and relentless Intentionality to get where you want to go. To set and achieve an ambitious goal: visualize, incrementalize, and Ignite. In chapter 4, we learned from multi-world record holders, Adrian Hayes and Annabelle Bond about goal setting and conquering Everest-sized challenges.

Create *your* aspirational Life Plan. It is an indispensable tool. Ten years from now, you will be grateful you made one. You can thank me later.

Work *your* money. An enriched life involves much more than money. Financial security just provides the foundation. Forget about The Number; focus on cash cows, financial fitness, and take control of your financial future. My journey to financial Independence was trial-and-error until I discovered how to work my money. HK Ang, profiled in chapter 7, emphasized debt reduction to accelerate financial freedom in under three years. The best time to build financial security is when you least need it.

Future-proof your financial security. We learned from Carla Jeffrey in chapter 6 about financial *in*security. Build financial security tier by tier in the image of an Aztec pyramid. Ensure you have a strong foundation. Advance toward your long-term financial objectives by following Annual Financial Plans. You can use Big Picture Budgeting to save time.

Ignite your plans. Set yourself up for success by deconstructing your goals into baby steps for quick wins. Use varied strategies to get going, and adjust the strategies to keep going. We learned from Airin Zainul in chapter 9 how to sustain motivation toward a multi-year quest using a variety of momentum techniques.

At work, take money out of the equation. Leverage your strengths and design your ideal job. Allow nonfinancial considerations to guide where and how much you work (or whether you work at all). Focus on the intangible benefits of work to improve career satisfaction. Innovate your career arc and fast-track optionality. We learned about job crafting from Jeremy Butler and Eleanor Rimbaud in chapter 10.

Adopt happiness habits. We do not find happiness; we create it. This requires the Five Ds of Discipline (Demarcate, Discern, Delegate, Daily Downtime, Detox), investing in the Essentials, and adding happiness boosters along the way. We learned from David Gething in chapter 11 how to self-Calibrate and integrate family, work, personal, and social priorities. Don't try to balance; integrate for cohesion and completeness.

Most importantly:

It's about Time. Change your relationship and commit to Time. Reject Time poverty; consider all the future possibilities and the abundance of Time going forward. Pay special attention to opportunity costs and Time creep.

CASE STUDY
ALEX STRAH

In the Introduction, you encountered my good friend, Alex Strah (pseudonym), who lost his job on the day that I relocated to the beach. This job loss was potentially catastrophic. But in just four months, in the worst job environment on record, he landed a refreshing role that paid *more* than his previous position.

Using the principles in this book, Alex Strah converted a layoff into an opportunity. This case study illustrates a real-life approach to integrating and implementing the ENRICH financial, career, and life strategies. It also demonstrates the durability and value of these concepts in an unhappy situation.

How did he do it?

Strah had plenty of concurrent issues to untangle:

1. Find the next job
2. Preserve cash and reduce his cost structure
3. Take care of his family
4. Maintain sanity

That is enough to wrap anyone around the axle.

Strah's first thoughts were dramatic. He envisioned a scenario of extreme frugality where he might have to "live in an unhappy cave for a year." He explains:

> This situation came out of nowhere. Suddenly, I had to find a new job. At the same time, I needed to soothe my family and decisively reduce our family expenses. That meant managing my wife and teenage daughters, who spend Dad's money. Somehow, I needed to find some personal balance. I could not afford for stress to derail me.

Job dislocations are commonplace; most professionals experience at least one. But this job loss coincided with a raging pandemic and an unemployment epidemic. Under the weight of these pressures, Strah's first instinct was to fly to Silicon Valley, talk to people, and look for another job in the same field. That's what he'd done in the past.

This layoff, however, was different. In his early fifties, Strah realized he could no longer afford to repeat past mistakes. He worried that without corrective action he might delay or jeopardize his retirement. He also understood this layoff presented an opportunity to reset and rethink everything.

Strah took a deep breath and flew to Phuket.

We spent a week together reading, discussing, and workshopping each draft chapter in this book. He resolved to take stock, get the fundamentals right, and create a plan *before* proceeding with the new job search.

Strah's first order of business was to know his numbers. Using the Big Picture Budgeting technique outlined in chapter 8, Strah analyzed his current financial situation. He explains:

> I have kept a detailed household budget for several years. Still, I never made the time to look at the numbers and recalibrate based on those numbers. Because I kept that budget, I had a false sense of security. I thought I was doing everything right.

This know-the-numbers exercise produced quite a surprise:

> When I reviewed last year's spending budget, I was shocked that I overspent my take-home earnings by about $70,000. This deficit deceives because my annual expenditures include paying down mortgage loans on multiple investment properties. As such, I paid down about this same amount on principal payments—something I never calculated previously—so net I saved nothing last year. That was a wake-up alarm.

Knowing the numbers also yielded a pleasant insight. After doing the math, Strah forecast the hurdle rate for financial freedom:

> By following through the bottom-up exercise to determine

my financial Independence target, I realized that I was not as far off as I thought. I realized that achieving my minimum threshold target could be achievable as a stretch goal in two to three years.

Following these insights and the financial fitness guidelines in chapter 6, Strah worked assiduously to reduce his cost structure. He focused on the big picture items, the things that move the needle. Living in one of the world's costliest cities, he concluded that it was far more cost-effective to rent than to own. This revelation was the key to reducing costs *and* increasing financial security. He explains:

> I then created a budget assuming worst case it takes twelve months to find my next full-time role. I also realized we needed to sell our principal residence and downsize. It alleviates the burden of having to earn high wages to pay all of my mortgage debts continually. I calculated a triple win. If I take the proceeds from selling our expensive home entirely and pay off my investment property mortgages, I will be debt-free. I will reduce my annual expenditures by more than 40 percent. And I will have some decent passive income from my investment properties!

He moved the recurring cost needle even further by off-loading a seldom-used club membership. He also took advantage of a government scheme during the COVID-19 crisis to defer mortgage payments, interest, and tax payments. These efforts reduced his monthly outflows by about half and enabled him to conserve cash during the job search. Together, these actions put him on a trajectory toward financial freedom, even while he was unemployed.

Strah also aggressively repositioned some investments. By knowing the numbers, he realized two critical vulnerabilities in his investment profile. First, a single position accounted for more than 20 percent of his total net worth, an uncomfortably high concentration of assets. Second, his index fund investments yielded very little cash flow. He repositioned these funds to generate some passive income that partially offset the loss of earned income. He also created an emergency cash fund from these liquid assets.

Strah actioned most of these financial maneuvers in approximately three weeks. Though counterintuitive, by investing the time upfront in analyzing and restructuring his financial situation, this substantially reduced stress from the job loss.

With this financial foundation and some passive income streams in place, he approached this job hunt quite differently than he had previous searches. Strah could afford to take some time to find the right professional opportunity, rather than jumping at the first offer, which would have meant a pay cut. That was a liberating insight that helped him avoid a costly mistake.

Strah also reflected on the unconventional strategy to take money out of the work equation from chapter 10. Previously he had always gravitated toward the most lucrative roles, in part because he had to bankroll a high-cost structure. With a clear path toward financial Independence, he could now evaluate potential jobs on the merit of the opportunity, and not on the compensation. This had a profound Impact on his conversations with various headhunters, venture capital investors, and employers.

Strah also focused on leveraging his strengths. He discovered his skillsets were valuable and transferable. Leveraging strengths gave him some latitude to look at related fields in his industry. "I'm quite pumped about this next phase in my career, and excited to do something new and different," he said.

In parallel with this financial and professional journey, Strah accelerated efforts toward his nonnegotiable and important priorities. He synchronized and merged these with his wife's aspirations. There was quite a bit of overlap, he happily learned. Together, they spent several weeks refining a one, three, and ten-year Life Plan. (Refer to Appendix VII, A Real-Life Life Plan.)

Although the job loss was a setback and he was uncertain when he would work again, Strah determined not to allow this speed bump to slow down his mid-to-long-term plans. His Life Plan combines a healthy mix of tactical and aspirational goals. For the current year, he resolved to use his unemployment downtime purposefully to spend quality time with his wife. Further out, his significant goals include relocating to another country. Recognizing the importance of having something to look forward to, he committed to treating weekends like mini-holidays in the short term. In the medium term, he determined to organize memorable annual family holidays.

He developed SMARTA goals for each near term high priority. To increase the probability of success, he adopted some success factors from chapter 9, specifically incrementalizing, writing down, and scheduling goals, and regular reviews.

Strah imposed time discipline and introduced some new routines, which immediately lifted the quality of his life and his relationships. He stripped down his calendar to the most critical matters. "The Time Audit" exercise in chapter 12 jolted him:

I realized that for years my color-coded calendar—work, personal and family—looked like a rainbow. By color coding, I thought I had balanced my life, but it was a false sense of balance. I had frequently double-booked appointments and on some days only had ten spare minutes in the whole day. Every day felt rushed. There was no time to think, or even say hello to people. Because of the insane Monday-Friday schedule, I was exhausted every weekend and so just vegged without enjoying that time off.

With a decluttered calendar, he started taking long walks with his wife, without the phone. He prioritized exercise and made it social, making sure to put fitness into his newly accommodative schedule. He now compartmentalizes his life the way David Gething does, focusing intently on each sphere at the appropriate time of day. Treating weekends like a vacation profoundly recharged his energy each week. Three-day weekends, even during the heat of the job search, were one of the best lifestyle changes he adopted. He adds:

I liked the "Magic Hour" exercise in chapter 11 on what I would do with a 25th hour every day. This extra hour would not be working one more hour each day. I would spend this extra hour on personal time for myself or with my family. This realization reinforced what matters most to me.

Lastly, with confidence in the future, he scheduled a family trip twelve months out to give him and his family something exciting to anticipate. He earmarked some funds in his budget for this fun activity. This planned vacation will be more modest than previous family trips. Still, he wants his family to have a good time together in a different environment. That is a nonnegotiable priority.

In reflecting on the ENRICH process, Strah confesses:

I am a classic workaholic. I work, then I work some more. I do not necessarily enjoy work. I work hard because of my family upbringing. I am wired to think that hard work translates into reaching my dreams of financial Independence faster. Now that I have done many of the basics in this book, including creating an achievable Life Plan, I'm clear on my goals. It really helps me focus.

One of the most valuable insights of ENRICH, Strah adds, is the importance of regular goal reviews. He explains:

Twelve years ago, I wrote down some goals and filed that piece of paper. Regular reviews are so obvious, yet this is something that I overlooked for many years. I have now set up calendar alerts to prevent this from happening anymore.

Strah's transformation was complete within two months. It began with getting the fundamentals in place first: understanding the numbers, creating fast financial flexibility, and identifying what is most important.

Strah tells me after adopting and following these practices, "I am much happier than I expected to be, given the circumstances. For the first time in a long time, I am excited and much more certain about the future."

What about that job search?

In the worst employment environment since the Great Depression, Strah pulled off a Hail Mary. Just four months after learning about his redundancy, he landed a new gig with an established startup. His new role involves significantly more revenue responsibility and compensation than his former position, in a refreshingly different IT sector from his previous four roles. "I am confident I can do well. It's a growing company. I inherit a strong team. I know how to do this," he tells me.

When the odds were against him, how did Strah find such a sweet role so quickly? He created his own luck. During a trip to the Bay Area, he accidentally ran into an acquaintance he had not seen in years. Several weeks later, that acquaintance heard about a job opening and immediately thought of Strah.

And how, exactly, did he create his own luck? Strah had a job search *plan* and forced himself to *follow-through* with the networking trip to the Bay Area even though he felt inclined to abort the trip at the last moment.

ENRICH triggered a mindset shift. He explains:

> My goal of financial Independence in a few years changes the game. I'm happy with my Life Plan and the goalposts on the horizon. It's satisfying that in just a few months, I already see a progression toward these goals, starting with this new job! This pause gave me time to reset and rebalance. Before, work was 100 percent of my life. Everything else was secondary. Well, no more.

A month into his new role, I check in with Strah to see how he's doing. "That layoff and ENRICH catalyzed everything," he jubilantly tells me, and continues:

> I am more structured, more disciplined, more focused, and much less stressed. And I'm sticking with this. I had procrastinated for years with my money. Now I'm doing something about it! I exercise, have a better outlook about the future, am balanced and grateful. Every Friday at 5 p.m. I close the

workweek. I look back to see what I accomplished. Then I plan the following week and identify goals across four buckets—personal finance, family, personal, and career. Then I enjoy the weekend and don't touch my computer until Monday morning.

In a short time, Alex Strah profoundly enriched his life.

DELICIOUS

If you have not yet created a Life Plan and an Annual Financial Plan, grab some paper and a pen and go to a quiet place. Please invest fifteen minutes in your enrichment by sketching out your highest personal, financial, and professional aspirations. Respect what comes top-of-mind, for these are usually among the truest priorities. You can access templates for the Life Plan and Annual Financial Plan in chapters 5 and 8, or at www.enrich101.com. These templates provide an initial starting point, which you can customize to reflect your circumstances.

These ENRICH strategies are not the only way to enrich life, of course. But they work. Together, they transform. Whether you follow any of these strategies or not, consider this: planfulness vastly boosts the probability of success. This applies to your life and financial goals and to any other aspiration. Investing the time to map your route will not only help you get where you want to go but will also accelerate the travel time. "Things take longer to happen than you think they will," writes Al Gore in *The New York Times*, "but then they happen much faster than you thought they could."

At the beginning of this book, I promised to do my best to make ENRICH worthy of your Time. My sincere hope is that ENRICH provides a practical, actionable framework to nurture life success and financial security. I hope the stories and strategies in these pages motivate you to proceed with relentless Intentionality toward what's most important.

Is this book helpful? If so, other readers and I would benefit from hearing about your ENRICH experience. Honest reviews help readers identify the best book for their needs. Please tell your friends, leave me a message at www.enrich101.com, or leave a review on Amazon books and Goodreads. I'd love to hear from you.

Let's be honest, folks: an enriched life requires hard work. But the rewards are *delicious*. The goal, after all, is not to have it all—but to Ignite all that matters.

May your days and years fully enrich with wealth in time, money, and meaning.

Todd Miller
Phang Nga, Thailand
June 30, 2020

BONUS CHAPTER

INHIBITORS

"Illegitimus non carborundum (Don't let the bastards grind you down)."

—LATIN PUN

"Things which matter most must never be at the mercy of things which matter least."

—JOHANN GOETHE

We've covered the six ENRICH life optimization strategies, and perhaps you have already noodled with a Life Plan and an Annual Financial Plan. This chapter tackles common inhibitors to putting ENRICH into practice.

INHIBITOR #1: WHERE DO I BEGIN?

The best place to start is to invest in the fundamentals, as Alex Strah did in chapter 13:

1. *Self:* Take care of yourself first. That is not selfish; it is pragmatic. You need to be in top form to support everyone depending

upon you. To take care of yourself, Essentialize (chapter 2) and get the biological fundamentals right—sleep, nutrition, exercise. Often when we feel deflated, the feeling manifests a deficiency in life's Essentials. Like tires, we need to inflate to keep in optimal condition.

2. *Family*: Then prioritize family. Take care of people and relationships first. As we've discussed, Interpersonal connectivity is the most influential life success factor.

3. *Invest in self-awareness*: ENRICH is the work of a lifetime. Understand the fundamentals: what you care about, what you want to accomplish, and your financial situation. There are no shortcuts. This groundwork creates the basis for everything else. To start, complete all the Take Action exercises in this book if you have not done so already. Focus on your Mission Statement (chapter 3), which will help define the core of the life you want.

4. *Finances*: Get cracking on your Annual Financial Plan (chapter 8). Make sure you are on a responsible trajectory toward financial security. This may be a years-long journey, so start it as soon as possible. As we have explored throughout this book, financial security provides the confidence to live life on your terms.

5. *Goals*: Tackle your Hierarchy of Priorities, and be gut sure of your conviction toward your priorities. Do not try to do everything at once. Determine what is most important or what will most Impact your enrichment. Incrementalize. Deconstruct a big goal into actionable increments you can assuredly achieve with effort. Ignite with a quick win that will energize you. Chapters 4 and 9 will help you set and Ignite compelling goals.

INHIBITOR #2: I'VE LOST MOMENTUM/FACED A SETBACK

Expect to veer off course. Obstacles are part of the journey. To quote a sage fortune cookie message, "When things go wrong, don't go with them."

How to regain momentum?

Recall what makes your endeavor essential. What is the Why? What are the positive outcomes of success, and what are the adverse consequences of failure?

Then diagnose how you strayed off course. This usually happens through one of three scenarios:

Setback. Sometimes events happen beyond your control. In 2020, while the world had other plans, the coronavirus pandemic exploded. Everyone and everything halted. When an external factor interrupts your trajectory, focus. Focus on what you can control, what you can accomplish, and what you need to do. Do not allow exogenous factors to distract from your Mission or become permanent hindrances. Often, a setback is just that—a delay, a timing issue. Sometimes, a setback requires a workaround solution. Whether the situation demands a new timeline or a workaround, your first step is to figure out how to reignite momentum.

Lost momentum. You simply lose energy. You skipped a day, and then another. Those two days became a week, and that week became a month. It happens to all of us, despite the best intentions. Restarting is a whole lot harder than stopping.

The most efficient way to regain momentum is to change your routine.

In chapter 9, we explored several success factors for achieving big goals. These include setting intermediate milestone goals for quick wins, creating catalysts and accountability mechanisms, surrounding yourself with like-minded people, and putting money on the line. Use a combination of these methods to change your routine and regain momentum. Consider even changing the techniques themselves. For instance, you can change the incentives—use punitive rewards like donating to a cause you vehemently oppose, instead of compensatory awards like treating yourself to some pampering. It is trial-and-error to figure out the right mix of incentives to sustain motivation.

There are various tools in the tool kit. Mix it up. Swap out the carrots and sticks. Remind yourself why this pursuit is essential. Quite often, modest tweaks to motivations or methods will do the trick.

By keeping the strategies fresh and varied, chances are you will be able to regain momentum with just a few tweaks and a little extra effort.

I completely lost it. I tried everything. I depleted the tool kit, and I just cannot get going again.

If this is the case, ask yourself these questions:

What circumstance changed in your life, and is this circumstance temporary or persistent? Have your priorities shifted? Might there be a work-around solution to accommodate this new circumstance? Is the change in circumstance an indefinite one, like a change in the health of a loved one?

Sometimes the best strategy for dealing with change, especially if a circumstance is not permanent, is to pause. Trying to do too much at once can be a frustrating and unhappy experience. It may be useful to take a break, simplify your life, and then pick back up with renewed vigor when you can (as long as this pause does not become an indefinite postponement).

This book is the result of that way of thinking. I prioritize family above everything else. While developing this book, life got in the way. I put the book on hiatus for over a year while I focused on family. Before I put the project on hiatus, I identified the date I would resume, and I put that commitment into the calendar. Moreover, I put money on the line and scheduled a writing workshop for the planned restart. Taking steps to resume at a specific future date enabled me to accept this pause and focus on the higher priority.

However, priorities do shift. It may be necessary, during one of your regular Life Plan check-ups, to start back at the beginning. Reevaluate what takes precedence and whether the goal you're struggling with remains a focus. If it does, then you will need to dig deep and figure out a way to tackle this priority very differently, since the status quo does not work.

If this priority no longer makes the shortlist, accept that and move on. Then focus on what *is* most important.

INHIBITOR #3: HOW DO I CREATE A LIFE PLAN FOR MY FAMILY? MY FAMILY MEMBERS HAVE DIFFERENT PRIORITIES.

Many professionals find creating a family Annual Financial Plan an easier task than creating a family Life Plan. The quick answer: highlight the commonalities. Ideally, there will be consensus within the family on nonnegotiable priorities. Common important now priorities should also factor into the plan. Focus on the goals on which the family aligns; otherwise, there will be no common ground for this Plan.

The family Life Plan can include allowances and mechanisms for the pursuit of individual passions. Within the plan's time frame, each family member can have space to pursue passion projects that may or may not involve other family members. The principle is, flexibility and reciprocity must exist for the Life Plan's durability.

INHIBITOR #4: ENRICH IS FUTURE-ORIENTED, BUT I TRY TO LIVE IN THE PRESENT. HOW DO I RECONCILE THIS?

ENRICH advances and embraces your most important current priorities. It is the opposite of living a deferred life by putting off the good stuff until you get that proverbial gold watch and retire. Nicholas Kristof, the Pulitzer-winning *New York Times* Opinion columnist, wrote about the secrets to success:

> The worst advice people give students is to spend the first third of their lives studying, the middle third making money, and the final third giving back. That would rob you for two-thirds of your life of meaning and fulfillment. If you dropped dead of a heart attack at 50, you'd be gnashing your teeth for all eternity.

My grandfather is a classic life deferrer. He worked his entire adult life as an engineer with the Eastman Kodak Company and retired in his early sixties with a pension right on schedule and a gold watch as a parting gift. For years, I heard about my grandparents' plan to visit Hawaii once my grandfather finally retired.

Unfortunately, my grandparents never fulfilled their dream to visit the Big Island. Family and health issues got in the way. The deferred plans evaporated.

ENRICH is all about focusing on the present and enjoying what life has to offer. It's about stepping away from the default setting *precisely* so that you can do this.

That said, while you are enjoying your present tense life, having a long-term plan is valuable for two reasons. First, it ensures you get where you want to go. Second, having something to look forward to contributes to happiness levels, especially during stressful periods.

Overcoming present bias *is* a challenge. The technique of reverse engineering incentives in chapter 9 will help you address this natural tendency to think and act short term.

INHIBITOR #5: I JUST CANNOT SAVE MONEY. FINANCIAL SECURITY IS NOT POSSIBLE FOR ME.

Do you have written financial goals? If not, write down a financial plan—this doubles the odds that you will achieve your financial targets, as we discussed in chapter 8. Give yourself this tactical advantage.

Then examine both sides of the money equation, income and expenses. Many people only focus on one side of the equation, either just trying to boost earnings or just managing nominal costs. To be effective, you must scrutinize both sides.

After that, follow the money. Understand your present spending and income habits. As a rule of thumb, necessities (including housing, food, and transportation) should account for about half of your take-home income. Discretionary spending, such as clothes and entertainment, should account for roughly a quarter of your take-home income, with savings accounting for the last quarter.

The best way to start saving is to take a baby step. Pick a savings rate you can manage. Whatever life stage you are in, there is always *some amount* you can save. Maybe it is only fifty dollars or 1 percent of your income to start. That is better than not saving at all. Sequester the savings. Then, after a while, take another baby step and grow the savings. One percent eventually becomes 2 percent, and if you keep at it, the savings can grow into something meaningful. Appendix III illustrates this principle over a working lifetime.

Once you start, make sure you pay yourself first. Vigorously enforce this principle. Save then spend. For best results, automate your savings every month to an off-limits account.

If you still cannot make ends meet, then you need to reexamine your cost structure ruthlessly. Scrutinize your top three expenditure categories, especially housing and transportation. You may need to downsize to satisfy long-term financial objectives.

In addition, you may need to change your cost structure radically.

If you live in an expensive coastal city, you might consider relocating to a less expensive area. While you may take a hit on income, you may significantly decrease your cost structure and improve your quality of life through geo-arbitrage.

If you want to think outside the box, consider an international move. As a long-term expatriate, I can attest that working abroad has the potential to enhance your savings and enrich your cultural and social life profoundly. Not only do you get to activate the eight Essentials, you can also expand your worldview.

Working abroad can fast-track financial security. Depending upon your location, a stint abroad can substantially lower your cost structure while enhancing your quality of life. I would never advocate relocating overseas for purely financial reasons. However, if an international lifestyle appeals to you, the financial perks of living abroad may be irresistible.

INHIBITOR #6: I'M TOO BUSY

Why are you so busy?

Distinguish between busyness and productivity. Busyness is a contemporary status symbol. We should not care about status symbols. Audit how you spend your time and determine whether or not this busyness is productive or even necessary (chapter 12).

Then, figure out how to practice the Five Ds outlined in chapter 11—especially the strategies to demarcate, discern, and delegate—to liberate your time.

You've done all that, and you're *still* super busy? Genuinely up-to-the-eyeballs busy with important stuff?

If you cannot subtract from your day, then add to your day.

The perverse nature of being super busy is that we often sacrifice what energizes us: Invigoration, Inspiration and Interpersonal connectivity. Sometimes the solution is to add more positive things to our day—to counteract the negatives—rather than to subtract from the day. For an enriched life, we need the eight Essentials, even if that means a busy person getting a little busier.

Take fitness as an example. When we are busy, we often feel exhausted. The time when we *most* need Invigoration is when our energy wanes. Pumping endorphins lifts energy levels and mood.

INHIBITOR #7: I AM AT THE TOP OF THE MOUNTAIN PROFESSIONALLY. I CAN'T GET OFF.

When you are at your professional peak, it is like standing at the edge of a cliff. How do you get off?

Jumping, such as going from peak performance to full retirement, can be a very frightening situation. So take the stairs. Plan a transition that gets you off the mountain in graduated milestone steps. A multi-year staircase to transition out of work might first involve a shift to 75 percent work, then a transition to 25 percent work (e.g., consulting and advising), before permanently stepping off the professional staircase.

The beauty of taking the stairs is you can climb up and down as you like, depending upon circumstances and interests.

This staircase solution can apply to any situation in which you encounter dramatic change. It is often more comfortable to take graduated steps than to take the plunge.

INHIBITOR #8: THESE WORK STRATEGIES ARE TOO RADICAL. THEY WON'T WORK AT MY COMPANY.

While I was working for the Hollywood studio, one colleague asked for a significant pay raise in a salary negotiation. His boss retorted, "You ask for more than I make!" The executive countered, quickly, "Well, it pushes up the bar for everyone."

Maybe Hollywood is an extreme example, but the principle holds.

The chances are high that your colleagues want the same things you do but are too afraid to ask. Consider business communication over weekends. Most people would rather not be bothered but play along because everyone else does. Why not change the conversation? Why not start a dialogue about demarcation? Most people would welcome a candid discussion about business expectations and etiquette because it would allow them to create some boundaries in their personal lives.

Just because your organization does not do something, do not let it deter you. I learned from my sabbatical request that sometimes you just need to ask. If the company rejects your proposal, what is the downside? Do you forfeit anything? Does the potential upside justify posing the question?

ENRICH: KEY TAKEAWAYS: INHIBITORS

There is a Zen proverb: "Obstacles do not block the path; they are the path." Throughout this book, we have discussed how to set goals and progress toward them. Along the way, you should expect some impediments on your journey to enrichment. Every challenge has a solution, and this chapter outlines solutions to overcome common obstacles to put ENRICH into practice.

- To start, invest in the fundamentals.
- If you get stuck, recall The Why, diagnose the setback, and focus on what you can control.
- To create a family Life Plan, highlight commonalities and allow for individual passions.
- Be unwilling to postpone what's most important.
- To save money, write down your goals and follow the money. Take a baby step to save *something*, then take another baby step; ruthlessly reconsider your cost structure.
- If you're too busy for the Essentials, add to your day rather than trying to subtract.

- Structure any major life transition as a staircase rather than a cliff.
- Sometimes you just need to ask—especially with "radical" ideas.

APPENDIX I

THE ENRICH TOOL KIT:
A CHEAT SHEET

ESSENTIALIZE *E* NARROW *N* REACH *R* IGNITE *I* CALIBRATE *C* HARNESS TIME *H*

STEP I: ESSENTIALIZE—THE EIGHT ESSENTIALS

- Interpersonal connectivity
- Independence
- Identity
- Intentionality
- Impact
- Integration
- Inspiration
- Invigoration

STEP II: NARROW

- ⓢ Mission
  - Amazon approach
  - Epitaph approach
- ⓢ Hierarchy of Priorities
  - ENRICH method: identify nonnegotiables
  - ABC method
  - Warren Buffett method
- ⓢ How to avoid the default setting
  - Take care of a personal priority first
  - Do not delay nonnegotiables
  - Make peace with your priorities

STEP III: REACH

- ⓢ SMARTA goals
  - Specific
  - Measurable
  - Accountable
  - Realistic
  - Timely
  - Authentic
- ⓢ To set a compelling goal
  - Visualize
  - Incrementalize
- ⓢ *Your* Aspirational Life Plan
- ⓢ The Life List
- ⓢ Cultivate cash cows
- ⓢ Financial Fitness
  - Know your numbers
  - Create a cash cushion
  - Save before you spend
  - Live below your means

- Eliminate debt
- Automate and find joy in saving
- Start early
- Always think TAKE-HOME income, net after taxes, and other expenses
- Consider arbitrage
- Visualize and incrementalize to build financial security—the Aztec model
- Big Picture Budgeting
- Annual Financial Plans

STEP IV: IGNITE

- Set up for success: write down and schedule goals
- Get started
  - Take a baby step
  - Incrementalize
  - Specificity
  - Immerse yourself
  - Create a catalyst
  - Rehearse the beginning
  - No fanfare, no fuss
  - Summon motivation sparks
- Keep going
  - Integrate, don't segregate
  - Add accountability
  - Schedule, create reminders and visual cues
  - Impose deadlines
  - Go public and social
  - Focus on what you can control
  - Aim for consistency, not perfection
  - Why and Why Not
  - Get some gratification

- Measure and Monitor
- Mix it up
- ⑤ Overcome the fear factor
- ⑤ Overcome present bias

STEP V: CALIBRATE

- ⑤ Work-hacking strategies
  - Take money out of the equation
  - Work fewer hours
  - Leverage your strengths
  - Craft your job, on your terms
  - "Help me help you"
  - Innovate your career arc
  - Create optionality
- ⑤ How to Essentialize:
  - Practice discipline—The Five Ds
    ◦ Demarcate
    ◦ Discern
    ◦ Delegate
    ◦ Daily Downtime
    ◦ Detox
  - Invest in the Essentials
    ◦ Interpersonal connectivity
    ◦ Invigoration
    ◦ Inspiration
  - Integrate
  - Add some happiness boosters
    ◦ Shared experiences
    ◦ Anticipation
    ◦ Vacations
    ◦ Unscheduled, unstructured time

STEP VI: HARNESS TIME

⑤ Create Time Wealth
- Pivot to abundance
- Be unwilling to postpone
- Simulate urgency
- Prioritize your Time expenditures
- Mind the opportunity costs
- Avoid Time creep

APPENDIX II

ELEVEN TAKE-ACTION EXERCISES

STEP II: NARROW STRATEGIES

- Craft Your Mission Statement (chapter 3)
- Build Your Hierarchy of Priorities (chapter 3)

STEP III: REACH STRATEGIES

- Convert Priority to Compelling Goal (chapter 4)
- Construct Your Life Plan (chapter 5)
- Build Your Financial Security (chapter 8)
- Build Your Annual Financial Plan (chapter 8)

STEP IV: IGNITE STRATEGIES

- Get Into Action (chapter 9)
- Vanquish the Fear Factor (chapter 9)

STEP V: CALIBRATE STRATEGIES

- ⑤ The Magic Hour (chapter 11)
- ⑤ Add What's Missing (chapter 11)

STEP VI: HARNESS TIME STRATEGIES

- ⑤ The Time Audit (chapter 12)

APPENDIX III

LONG-TERM SAVINGS MODEL

This model demonstrates that modest levels of saving can build significant wealth over time—especially if you start early.

LONG-TERM SAVINGS MODEL

Assumptions

Initial savings rate: 5.00% | Growth in savings: 1.00% | Earnings on investments: 5.00%

YEAR	AGE	SALARY	SAVINGS				TAKE HOME	
			RATE	AMOUNT	EARNINGS	CUMULATIVE		
1	22	40,000	5%	2,000		2,000	38,000	
2	23	41,600	6%	2,496	100	4,596	39,104	2.90%
3	24	43,264	7%	3,028	230	7,854	40,236	2.90%
4	25	44,995	8%	3,600	393	11,847	41,395	2.90%
5	26	46,794	9%	4,211	592	16,650	42,583	2.90%
6	27	48,666	10%	4,867	833	22,350	43,800	2.90%
7	28	50,613	11%	5,567	1,117	29,034	45,045	2.80%
8	29	52,637	12%	6,316	1,452	36,803	46,321	2.80%
9	30	54,743	13%	7,117	1,840	45,759	47,626	2.80%
10	31	56,932	14%	7,971	2,288	56,018	48,962	2.80%
11	32	59,210	15%	8,881	2,801	67,700	50,328	2.80%
12	33	61,578	16%	9,853	3,385	80,938	51,726	2.80%
13	34	64,041	17%	10,887	4,047	95,872	53,154	2.80%
14	35	66,603	18%	11,989	4,794	112,654	54,614	2.70%
15	36	69,267	19%	13,161	5,633	131,447	56,106	2.70%
16	37	72,038	20%	14,408	6,572	152,427	57,630	2.70%
17	38	74,919	21%	15,733	7,621	175,781	59,186	2.70%
18	39	77,916	22%	17,142	8,789	201,712	60,774	2.70%
19	40	81,033	23%	18,638	10,086	230,435	62,395	2.70%
20	41	84,274	24%	20,226	11,522	262,183	64,048	2.60%
21	42	87,645	25%	21,911	13,109	297,203	65,734	2.60%
22	43	91,151	26%	23,699	14,860	335,762	67,452	2.60%
23	44	94,797	27%	25,595	16,788	378,146	69,202	2.60%
24	45	98,589	28%	27,605	18,907	424,658	70,984	2.60%
25	46	102,532	29%	29,734	21,233	475,625	72,798	2.60%
26	47	106,633	30%	31,990	23,781	531,396	74,643	2.50%
27	48	110,899	31%	34,379	26,570	592,345	76,520	2.50%
28	49	115,335	32%	36,907	29,617	658,869	78,428	2.50%
29	50	119,948	33%	39,583	32,943	731,395	80,365	2.50%
30	51	124,746	34%	42,414	36,570	810,379	82,332	2.40%
31	52	129,736	35%	45,408	40,519	896,305	84,328	2.40%
32	53	134,925	36%	48,573	44,815	989,693	86,352	2.40%
33	54	140,322	37%	51,919	49,485	1,091,097	88,403	2.40%
34	55	145,935	38%	55,455	54,555	1,201,108	90,480	2.30%
35	56	151,773	39%	59,191	60,055	1,320,354	92,581	2.30%
36	57	157,844	40%	63,137	66,018	1,449,510	94,706	2.30%
37	58	164,157	41%	67,304	72,475	1,589,290	96,853	2.30%
38	59	170,724	42%	71,704	79,464	1,740,458	99,020	2.20%
39	60	177,553	43%	76,348	87,023	1,903,828	101,205	2.20%

Courtesy of Ken Jacquin

APPENDIX IV

COMMON ASSET CLASS INVESTMENTS TO GENERATE CASH COWS

Real Estate: Among all asset classes, real estate best supports the ENRICH philosophy. Refer to Appendices V and VI.

Dividend stocks/funds: Look for funds/ETFs with attractive and consistently growing yield. Consider a fund that targets companies with a track record of increasing dividends.

Preferred stocks: Often overlooked, these equities can provide a dependable source of yield in low interest-rate environments. Preferred shares are a hybrid between stocks and bonds. They typically pay more than US treasuries, and offer more safety than ordinary shares, since preferred shareholders get priority on distributions.

High-grade corporate bond funds/ETFs, especially short to Intermediate duration (five to ten years): These are investment-grade corporate bonds. Be wary about the so-called junk bonds, which carry high yields to compensate for low credit quality. These companies are often highly levered, and in a market dislocation, junk bonds typically behave like equities.

Fixed income: Explore a broadly diversified bond fund that blends different types of government and investment-grade corporate issues, plus commercial mortgage-backed securities and other debt.

Exchange-traded bonds: These are individual bonds that trade on stock exchanges, with the yield on investment-grade offerings typically higher (in some cases, two or three times higher) than Treasury yields. The return is higher because issuers can call the bonds at par value at any point five years or later after issuance. However, bond interest taxes at ordinary income levels, rather than as dividend income.

Municipal bonds: Munis offer lower yields than other bonds. However, always look at returns after-tax. Munis merit some allocation for high tax bracket investors, especially those who live in high-tax states. Munis generate income that is exempt from Federal taxes, and generally from state taxes in the state issuing the bond.

Closed-end funds: These funds are usually levered 30-40 percent at institutional rates, which boosts yield. However, these funds have a fixed number of shares that trade each day. As a result, there may be a discount or premium to the value of the underlying holdings, and these funds may be less liquid than other types of funds. Closed-end municipal funds are an overlooked sub-category of munis, and offer substantially better after-tax yield, sometimes nearly double the return on municipals.

Annuities: Annuities provide lifetime income. Historically, several drawbacks have limited their appeal. Annuities are not inflation-adjusted, and they can be complicated and costly. However, all this is changing, which may make annuities a more viable option to engineer lifetime income going forward. The SECURE Act of 2019 relaxes some rules governing annuities in retirement plans such as 401(k)s. Moreover, companies such as BlackRock, the world's largest money manager, are getting in on the annuity action. Watch this space.

Charitable gift annuities: These under-the-radar annuities may have a role for investors seeking to multitask their investments. American educational institutions and other nonprofits typically offer these charitable gift annuities. They provide fixed lifelong payments, favorable annuity rates, tax benefits, and the opportunity to contribute to a worthy cause.

This list excludes two asset classes. Venture capital is not a prospective asset class for cash cows. VC investing, either in your own company or someone else's, can create real wealth. But such investments, especially early-stage companies, can drain cash as much as they can generate income. Similarly, gold, oil, commodities, and undeveloped land do not generate cash flow and therefore exclude from this list. Focus instead on productive, cash-producing assets.

APPENDIX V

WHY REAL ESTATE ENRICHES

Real estate is the most efficient asset class to generate passive, recurring, predictable, automatic tax-friendly cash flows because of the following factors:

Tangible Assets: Single-family homes, apartment buildings, condominiums, and commercial buildings are real assets.

Appreciation: The priority is cash flow, and real estate delivers tax-advantaged cash flow. As a bonus, real estate has also been historically one of the best asset classes for long-term capital appreciation.

Rising Demand: Since 2008-9, owning a home has become less critical to the American dream. According to Yardeni Research, since 2008-9, one-third of would-be homeowners opt to rent instead of buy. Because of this demand curve shift, the national median rent hit an all-time high in 2019, according to *The Wall Street Journal.*

Inflation-Protected Cash Flow: Generally, rents rise as inflation rises.

Exponential Wealth Creation: If you finance, your tenants will pay off your debt. If you do not finance, rental revenue streams can fund future acquisitions.

Long-Term Focus: You can dump stocks or bonds in an emotional instant. The friction and illiquidity in buying and selling real estate force a long-term focus. Real estate, not stocks, is the preferred long-term investment asset class in the United States, according to Bankrate.

Control: Unlike capital markets, in which you're along for the ride, you can exert 100 percent influence over your direct real estate investments. You can choose whether to rent long term or short term, whether to sell, and whether to add value. With real estate, you create more optionality.

Tax Advantages: The United States tax code favors real estate in some tangible ways:

Depreciation: The ability to deduct depreciation, a non-cash expense, from rental income is HUGE, as Donald Trump might say. During the October 2016 Presidential debate, he proclaimed, "I love depreciation!"

Capital Gains: Through a mechanism called the 1031 exchange, it is possible to defer capital gains taxes on real estate appreciation when exchanging like-for-like properties.

FICA: There is no payroll tax on rental income.

One More Sweetener: As a real estate professional, you can claim real estate losses—including losses due entirely to depreciation—to offset other income. To qualify, you cannot hold a full-time job doing something else, or have more than $125,000 annual income.

This example illustrates the compounding power of these dramatic tax advantages:

Step 1: Purchase a real estate asset. All expenses to operate and manage the property can deduct from rental income.

Step 2: Write off the depreciation of the building over 27.5 years.

Step 3. Tax loss. Although the property generates positive cash flow, after depreciation, the real estate produces a tax loss. In other words, rental income tax-defers. Tax losses carry forward, and, depending upon your circumstances, may offset other income.

Step 4: Defer capital gains. When the property sells through the 1031 process, the capital gains defer and reset with the replacement property.

Step 5: Repeat the process.

American inheritance laws respect these taxation benefits. The 1031 exchange mechanism allows heirs to defer capital gains taxes. When they inherit the property, its value steps up to fair market, thereby sidestepping the capital gains taxes on the property's appreciation. Real estate is thus a compelling means to create and transfer generational wealth. Wherever you invest, be sure to understand the tax laws, which can dynamically change.

APPENDIX VI

REAL ESTATE INVESTMENT STRATEGIES TO GENERATE CASH COWS

To create real estate cash cows, you'll need to address four issues:

1. Where
2. What
3. How
4. Debt

WHERE

Real estate is about location, location, location. Prime locations for real estate investing may surprise you. Consider these criteria for promising income property markets:

- Long-term population growth
- Long-term job growth
- Rising rental demand and prices (in other words, no over-supply)

- ⑤ Home prices relative to incomes
- ⑤ Tax/cost friendliness
- ⑤ Livability (is this a city people want to move to, or from?)
- ⑤ Education and skill of the workforce
- ⑤ Economic diversification (is the city too heavily reliant on a single industry or company?)
- ⑤ Resilience to economic shock

Geographically, focus on markets with robust *net* rental demand and healthy yields, where plenty of real people have plenty of real jobs. *These markets will likely be unsexy and investors may overlook them.* For income properties, I encourage you to look beyond the coastal cities at locations that consistently have population and job growth prospects. Be wary of so-called "hot" investment markets.

In July 2019, *Business Insider* collaborated with Zillow to survey the one hundred largest cities with the highest growth in one-bedroom rents. The locations may surprise you. Cities in the southern and western parts of the US make up the majority of the top twenty-five markets. Indianapolis, Orlando, Oklahoma City, Fort Worth, Lexington, Tucson, and other midsize cities like these have the fastest-growing rents in the country.

In determining location, strip away any emotion. This investment is to generate dependable, recurring income. Be clear on this purpose, and do not mix pleasure with business. Under no circumstance should you confuse a vacation or weekend property with a 100 percent income-generating strategy. (If you opt for a vacation property and rent it out to defray the running costs, recognize this as a lifestyle decision, not an investment strategy.)

WHAT

There are many types of real estate cash flow strategies:

Direct Investments. Purchase and then lease single or multifamily homes, or commercial properties. Single-family homes are simpler to finance, and tenants pay all the utilities. Investments in single-family homes are also easier to exit if you do not buy and hold for the long haul.

Indirect investments. There are many vehicles for passive real estate investing through third parties:

· Real Estate Investment Trusts (REITs) specialize and own a particular type of real estate. REIT holdings include office towers, hotels, shopping complexes, apartment buildings, nursing homes, warehouses, and even storage facilities. Ninety percent of REIT earnings pass through to owners through dividends. REITs are pure passive investments; many tend to concentrate on major metro areas. There are two types of REITs: publicly traded and nontraded. Publicly traded REITs have easy liquidity and can be bought and sold like stocks. This means they also behave like stocks. Nontraded REITs are less liquid and less volatile. Prominent sponsors of such nontraded REITs include Blackstone Group and Starwood Capital.
· Private market investing, such as private equity real estate.
· Fintech crowdsourcing platforms, such as Crowdstreet, Fundrise, Realcrowd, and Cadre. Yes, you can own a small slice of a skyscraper. These platforms focus on commercial properties—multifamily, retail, office, hotel, industrial. Crowdstreet, for example, aims to bring institutional-quality deals to individual investors and offers the flexibility of directly investing in a specific opportunity or

a portfolio. These investments are 100 percent passive, but they do not have the liquidity features of traded REITs. These platforms offer diversification and the benefit of professional expertise. Some crowdfunders offer liquidity programs, after say five years, or impose a penalty on withdrawals after less than five years. Fintech firms such as JWB, Real Estate Capital, and Roofstock focus on single-family homes. These firms slice the ownership of single-family homes to cater to entry-level investors. If you are starting in real estate investing, these fintech platforms might be a place to get some initial experience. For any investment, conduct due diligence, including scrutinizing sponsor historical performance.

· Debt funds. The current restrictive lending environment creates a credit market gap for short-term real estate loans. Debt funds bridge this gap and can generate stable, passive monthly income—so long as there are no defaults and the loan-to-value threshold is moderate. Be sure to invest only in high-quality funds secured by first liens on the underlying real assets in the event of a default. Generally, the tax benefits of investing in debt are not as attractive as real estate equity. Distributions on debt usually tax as interest. They do not offer any depreciation benefits, since the debt fund does not own the underlying property, except in default.

HOW

You may think there is no way you can afford to invest directly in real estate. Two tactics—house hacking and condominium conversion—may alter this perception and present a realistic opportunity for beginner real estate investors.

House hacking offers an enticing starter solution by giving you a place to live—often, rent-free—*and* to engineer some rental income. To house hack, buy a duplex, triplex, or four-unit complex and live in one of the units. Rent out the others.

Condominium conversion is a variation of house hacking. With condo conversion, buy a multifamily property (typically two to four units). Rent them out. Then later sell off the units individually.

No matter how you invest, aim to achieve sufficient scale and diversification such that you are not overly reliant upon any single property or position. In the event that the property remains vacant for a while or requires maintenance expenses, cash flow from other properties can smooth the lumpiness in revenues and expenditures.

One real estate strategy I do *not* recommend is the fix-and-flip approach popularly portrayed on TV. Fix-and-flipping relies on capital gains rather than cash flow and is highly speculative. Speculation undermines financial security. I know many house flippers who have lost their pants sinking capital to rehabilitate homes that don't sell.

Whatever method you choose, do your homework.

DEBT

Capital requirements deter some prospective real estate investors. This brings us to the topic of debt. Recall from chapter 6 how eliminating consumer debt is crucial to fiscal fitness. This refers to credit card balances and car loans. What about investment debt, such as a mortgage on an income property?

Personally, I eschew all forms of debt. However, there are compelling financial benefits to leverage, especially when the cost of capital is low. If you choose to add leverage to start or to build a real estate portfolio, make sure you have holding power in the long run. Also, avoid bubbly, investor-popular real estate markets. Too much debt can destroy financial security in a flash.

In thinking about what's right for you, configure investment debt and equity to get to your targeted cash flow and to ensure an acceptable level of diversification. The goal is peace-of-mind and an enriched life. The optimal mix of debt and diversification is a personal decision based on individual comfort levels and risk tolerances. Do what will help you sleep well, so as not to worry about having too much debt or too little diversification.

APPENDIX VII

A REAL-LIFE LIFE PLAN

LIFE PLAN

Deepest Values: Family First // Enjoy Life Experiences // Explore the World

Mission: Be passionate about life experiences, commit to family for life and to deep friendships, and above all never settle for average

	2020, age 53	2022, age 55	2030, age 63
THE BIG THING:	Enjoy Life with Spouse	Financial Independence	Prepare for Advanced Age
TOP PRIORITIES:	Achieve balanced life from this year forward (and get used to it)	Enjoy time with spouse, loving close family	Enjoy time with spouse, loving close family
	Maintain health (particularly with COVID-19)	Kids achieving succes at Uni	Kids having happy careers & families
	Work towards getting a meaningful full-time job	Be successful at my job (from my boss's view)	Time and $$$ to travel extensively
	Be happy and positive at all times	Start planning for retirement	
FINANCIAL:	Re-balance & optimize our financial portfolio	Achieve financial security	Financially secure for future
	Sell primary residence	$____K net passive recurring cash flow by 12/31/21	
	Sell underperforming or unused assets and reduce spending	$____MM net worth	
		$____K net savings by 2021	
		Be debt free	
PROFESSIONAL:	Land job that I really enjoy, and can meaningfully contribute	Invest in 2nd startup	Become trusted advisor to startups or companies
	Be a better leader (ex. more empathy, more humor)	Get involved in startup community	Have 2 meaningful board roles
	Don't work on weekends		
	Help ____and____startups		
FAMILY:	Treat weekends like mini-holidays (something to look forward to)	Treat every weekend like a holiday	Retire before 60 in a different country
	Ensure kids' happiness	Have the best loving relationship with spouse	Treat every day like a holiday
	Be a parent kids can talk to	Prepare younger daughter for college	Have the best loving relationship with family
	Replace health insurance providers	Prepare older daughter for successful career	Epic and memorable annual family trips
	Have more fun and better communication with wife	Epic and memorable annual family trips	Loving close family
	Build respected relationship with kids	Loving close family	
QUALITY OF LIFE/ ENRICHMENT:	Complete Yale's "The Science of Well-Being" course	Enjoy annual holidays with friends	Live in Europe at least a year
	Aim for 1 family trip this year (when it's safe to travel again)	Be a good friend and accessible	Learn something new every day about the world
	Monthly connection with friends	Travelled to more than 50 countries	Attend Superbowl, Wimbledon, March Madness, World Series, NBA Championship, Olympics
			Travelled to more than 75 countries
HEALTH/FITNESS:	Maintain fitness & health: 150 min/week & daily vitamins	Maintain fitness I had at 40	Maintain fitness I had at 40
	Weekly fitness training with family		

REFERENCES

CHAPTER 1

Burn-Callendar, Rebecca, "It's Official: Most people are miserable at work," *The Telegraph*, September 18, 2015.

Cohen, Patricia, "Straggling in a Good Economy, and Now Struggling in a Crisis," *The New York Times*, April 16, 2020.

Fuhrmans, Vanessa, "Female Factor: Women Drive the Labor Force Comeback," *The Wall Street Journal*, March 1, 2019.

"Global Generations: A global study of work-life challenges across generations," *EY*, 2015. https://www.ey.com/ Publication/vwLUAssets/Global_generations_study/$FILE/ EY-global-generations-a-global-study-on-work-life-challenges-across-generations.pdf.

Schwartz, Nelson D. et al, "How Bad Is Unemployment? 'Literally, Off the Charts,'" *The New York Times*, May 8, 2020.

"U.S. Financial Health Pulse 2019 Trends Report,"

Financial Health Network, 2019. https://s3.amazonaws.com/cfsi-innovation-files-2018/wp-content/uploads/2019/12/16161507/2019-Pulse-Report-FINAL_1205.pdf.

CHAPTER 2

Epley, Nicholas, interview in "The Science of Well Being Course," Yale University/Coursera.

Hershfield, Hal and Mogilner, Cassie., "What Should You Choose: Time or Money," *The New York Times*, September 9, 2016.

Jebb, Andrew T. et al, "Happiness, income, income satiation and turning points around the world," *Nature Human Behavior*, January 2018.

Kahneman, Daniel and Deaton, Angus, "High income improves evaluation of life but not emotional well-being, Proceedings of the National Academy of Sciences of the United States of America," September 21, 2010.

Mineo, Liz, "Good Genes Are Nice, But Joy is Better," *The Harvard Gazette*, April 11, 2017.

Park, Nansook; Park, Myungsook; and Peterson, Christopher; "When Is the Search for Meaning Related to Life Satisfaction," *Applied Psychology: Health and Well Being*, 2010.

Reynolds, Gretchen, "A Single Session of Exercise Alters 9,815 Molecules in Our Blood," *The New York Times*, June 10, 2020.

Seligman, Martin E. P., "Flourish: A Visionary New

Understanding of Happiness and Well-Being," New York: Free Press, 2011.

"Social Relationships and Mortality Risk: A Meta-analytic Review," *PLoS Medicine*, July 27, 2010.

Vozza, Stephanie, "Personal Mission Statements of 5 Famous CEOs (And Why You Should Write One Too), *Fast Company*, February 25, 2014.

CHAPTER 4

Murphy, Mark, "Neuroscience Explains Why You Need to Write Down Your Goals If You Actually Want to Achieve Them," *Forbes*, April 15, 2018.

Newland, Stephen, "The Power of Accountability," Association for Financial Counseling and Planning Education," Quarter 3, 2018.

Orlick, Terry and Partington, John, "Mental Links to Excellence," *Sports Psychologist*, June 1988.

Sikes, Timothy, "6 Habits Longtime Millionaires Rely On To Stay Rich," *Entrepreneur*, May 10, 2018.

Wiese, B.S., "Successful pursuit of personal goals and subjective well-being," In B.R. Little, K. Salmela-Aro, & S.D. Phillips (Eds.), *Personal Project Pursuit: Goals, Action and Human Flourishing*, 2007.

Worrall, Simon, "Why K2 Brings Out the Best and Worst in Those Who Climb It," *National Geographic*, December 13, 2015.

CHAPTER 6

Akala, Adedayo, "More big companies are talking about permanent work-from-home positions," CNBC, May 1, 2020.

Becker, Sam, "How Much Money Does the Average American Need to Feel Financially Secure?" cheatsheet.com, December 7, 2017.

Board of Governors of the Federal Reserve System, "Report on the Economic Well Being of U.S. Households in 2018," May 2019.

Browning, Chris; Guo, Tao; Cheng, Yuanshan; and Finke, Michael; "Spending in Retirement: Determining the Consumption Gap," *Journal of Financial Planning*, April 2016.

Clinginsmith, David, "Negative emotions, income, and welfare: Causal estimates from the PSID," *Journal of Economic Behavior & Organization*, October 2016.

Eisenberg, Richard, "Is Working From Home The Future of Work?," *Forbes*, April 10, 2020.

Gillers, Heather; Tergesen, Anne; and Scism, Leslie; "A Generation of Americans Is Entering Old Age the Least Prepared in Decades," *The Wall Street Journal*, June 22, 2018.

Gosseilin, Peter, "If You're Over 50, Chances Are the Decision to Leave a Job Won't be Yours," *ProPublica*, December 28, 2018.

Harrison, David, "Lack of Savings Worsens the Pain of the Coronavirus Downturn," *The Wall Street Journal*, April 15, 2020.

Hill, Catey, "I'm 56 and unemployed, but have $100,000 to live off until I find a job. Where should I put this money?" *MarketWatch*, December 7, 2019.

Howard, Cooper and Williams, Rob, "Beyond the 4 percent Rule: How Much Can You Spend in Retirement?" https://www.schwab.com/resource-center/insights/content/beyond-4-rule-how-much-can-you-safely-spend-retirement.

Jebb, Andrew T; Tay, Louis; Diener, Ed; and Oishi, Shigehiro; "Happiness, income satiation and turning points around the world," *Nature Human Behavior*, January 8, 2018.

Langlois, Shawn, "Planning for retirement: Check out one of the 'scariest charts in human history,'" *MarketWatch*, November 30, 2016.

Mattioli, Dana and Putzier, Konrad, "When It's Time to Go Back to the Office, Will It Still Be There?" *The Wall Street Journal*, May 16, 2020.

Pinsker, Joe, "Who Actually Feels Satisfied about Money," *The Atlantic*, July 21, 2019.

"Retirement Security Amid COVID-19: The Outlook of Three Generations," Transamerica Institute, May 2020, https://transamericacenter.org/docs/default-source/retirement-survey-of-workers/tcrs2020_sr_retirement_security_amid_covid-19.pdf.

Social Security Administration, Benefits Planner—Life Expectancy, https://www.ssa.gov/planners/lifeexpectancy.html.

Sorkin, Andrew Ross, "Mark Zuckerberg Rethinks the Office," Dealbook, *The New York Times*, May 22, 2020.

CHAPTER 7

Andrews, Jeff, "How A Recession Could Impact The Housing Market," *Curbed*, January 10, 2019.

Brandt, Libertina, "The 25 US cities where rent is increasing the fastest, ranked," *Business Insider*, July 4, 2019.

Carpenter, Julia, "Your Parents' Financial Advice Is (Kind Of) Wrong," *The Wall Street Journal*, September 13, 2019.

Hoffman, Liz and Marcelo, Prince, "The Month Coronavirus Felled American Business," *The Wall Street Journal*, April 4, 2020.

Kusisto, Laura, "Investors Are Buying More of the US Housing Market Than Ever Before," *The Wall Street Journal*, June 20, 2019.

NMHC Rent Payment Tracker, National Multifamily Housing Council, https://www.nmhc.org/research-insight/nmhc-rent-payment-tracker/.

Royal, James, "Real Estate is Back as American's favorite Long Term Investment," Bankrate, July 17, 2019, https://www.bankrate.com/investing/financial-security-july-2019/.

Parker, Will, "Nearly a Third of Apartment Renters Didn't Pay April Rent," *The Wall Street Journal*, April 8, 2020.

Royal, James, "Real Estate is Back as American's favorite Long

Term Investment," Bankrate, July 17, 2019, https://www.bankrate. com/investing/financial-security-july-2019/.

Tangermann, Victor, "The Earth is Standing Still During the Pandemic. Literally." Futurism, April 3, 2020.

CHAPTER 8

Updegrave, Walter, "You're More Likely to Retire Wealthy If you DO This One Thing," *Money*, July 18, 2017.

CHAPTER 9

"Daily weighing may be the key to losing weight," American Heart Association, November 5, 2018.

DeSteno, David, "The Only Way to Keep Your Resolutions," *The New York Times*, December 29, 2017.

Matthews, Gail. Goals research study, Dominican University of California, 2015, https://www.dominican.edu/academics/lae/ undergraduate-programs/psych/faculty/assets-gail-matthews/ researchsummary2.pdf.

Newland, Stephen, "The Power of Accountability," Association for Financial Counseling and Planning Education," Quarter 3, 2018.

Wissman, Barrett, "An Accountability Partner Makes You Vastly More Likely to Succeed," *Entrepreneur* Magazine, March 20, 2018.

CHAPTER 10

Achor, Shawn et al., "9 out of 10 People are Willing to Earn Less Money to DO More Meaningful Work," *Harvard Business Review*, November 6, 2018.

Cutter, Chip, "She Took a Two Year Break In Her Career. Now She's CEO," *The Wall Street Journal*, October 11, 2019.

Drucker, Peter F., "Managing Yourself," *Harvard Business Review*, March-April 1999.

Eadicicco, Lisa, "Microsoft experiments with a 4-day workweek, and productivity jumped by 40 percent," *Business Insider*, November 4, 2019.

"Employee Job Satisfaction and Engagement: Revitalizing a Changing Workforce," *The Society For Human Resource Management*, page 33, 2016.

"From Positivity to Productivity: Exposing The Truth Behind Workplace Happiness," Wrike, May 2019, https://cdn.wrike.com/ebook/2019_US_Happiness_Index_Compensation.pdf.

How many productive hours in a workday? Just 2 hours and 23 minutes ...," www.vouchercloud.com, https://www.vouchercloud.com/resources/office-worker-productivity.

Kantor, Jodi and Streitfeld, David, "Inside Amazon: Wrestling Big Ideas In a Bruising Workplace," *The New York Times*, August 15, 2015.

Kraft, Sharyl, "Companies are facing an Employee Burnout Crisis," CNBC, August 11, 2018.

Lavy, Shiri and Littman-Ovadia, Hadassah, "My Better Self: Using Strengths at Work and Work Productivity, Organizational Citizenship Behavior, and Satisfaction," *Journal of Career Development*, February 25, 2016.

Lynch, Shana, "Why Your Workplace Might Be Killing You," Insights by Stanford Business, February 23, 2015.

Mattioli, Dana, "Senior Amazon Executive to Take a Year Off," *The Wall Street Journal*, July 31, 2019.

Muir, William M. and Wilson, David Sloan, "When the Strong Outbreed the Weak: An Interview with William Muir," The Evolution Institute, July 11, 2016.

Organization for Economic Co-Operation and Development (OECD), Labour Force Statistics, Average Annual Hours Actually Worked Per Worker, 2018, https://stats.oecd.org/Index. aspx?DataSetCode=ANHRS#.

"Our Study on the Elusive Work-Life Balance," Joblist. com, November 26, 2019, https://www.joblist.com/trends/ the-elusive-work-life-balance#SID-1.

Pink, Dan, "Drive: The Surprising Truth About What Motivates Us," 2009.

CHAPTER 11

"Americans Have More Free Time Than Generally Recognized," Rand Corporation, October 28, 2019.

Bezos, Jeff, "Why Getting 8 Hours of Sleep is Good for Amazon Shareholders," Thrive Global, November 30, 2016.

Dunn, Elizabeth and Norton, Michael, "Happy Money: The Science of Happier Spending," Simon and Schuster Paperbacks, 2013.

Emmons, Robert A., "Thanks! How the New Science of Gratitude Can Make You Happier," Houghton Mifflin Co., 2007.

"Exercise: 7 benefits of regular physical activity," The Mayo Clinic. https://www.mayoclinic.org/healthy-lifestyle/fitness/in-depth/exercise/art-20048389#:~:text=Regular percent20physical percent20activity percent20can percent20improve,energy percent20to percent20tackle percent20daily percent20chores.

Gillen JB, Martin BJ, MacInnis MJ, Skelly LE, Tarnopolsky MA, et al. "Twelve Weeks of Sprint Interval Training Improves Indices of Cardiometabolic Health Similar to Traditional Endurance Training despite a Five-Fold Lower Exercise Volume and Time Commitment," PLOS ONE 11(4): e0154075., 2016. https://doi.org/10.1371/journal.pone.0154075.

Holes, Cassie Magilner et al., "Treat Your Weekend Like A Vacation," *Harvard Business Review* Ascend, 2019.

Piferi, Rachel L. and Lawler, Kathleen A., "Social Support and Ambulatory Blood Pressure: An Examination of Both Receiving and Giving," *International Journal of Psychophysiology*, November 2006.

Schroeder, Alice, "The Snowball: Warren Buffett and The Business of Life," Bloomsbury Publishing, 2009.

Suttie, Jill, "Why Curious People Have Better Relationships," *Greater Good Magazine*, May 31, 2017.

Whillans, Ashley V. et al, "Buying time promotes happiness." Proceedings of the National Academy of Sciences of the United States of America," June 13, 2017.

White, Matthew P. et al., "Spending at Least 120 minutes A Week in Nature is Associated with Good Health and Well Being," Scientific Reports, June 13, 2019.

CHAPTER 12

"30 Surprising Facts About How We Spend Our Time," MSN, April 5, 2015.

Darley, John M. and Batson, C. Daniel, "From Jerusalem to Jericho: A Study of Situational and Dispositional Variables in Helping Behavior," *Journal of Personal and Social Psychology*, 1973.

"Finland to give dads same parental leave as mums," BBC News, February 5, 2020.

Fottrel, Quintin," People spend most of their waking hours staring at screens," MarketWatch, August 4, 2018.

Furniss, Tracey, "Why climber Annabelle Bond believes discipline is the key to happiness and success," *South China Morning Post*, January 5, 2020.

Mpgilner, Cassie, "It's time for happiness," Current Opinion in Psychology, vol. 26, April 2019.

Sanderson, Catherine A., "Why Are the Finns So Happy? Three Lessons We Can Learn," *Psychology Today*, April 25, 2020.

Hall, Trish, "What Does the Good Life Look Like Now?" *The New York Times*, April 18, 2020.

Twenge, Jean M, "The Sad State of Happiness in the United States and the Role of Digital Media," World Happiness Report, 2019, https://worldhappiness.report/ed/2019/the-sad-state-of-happiness-in-the-united-states-and-the-role-of-digital-media/.

World Happiness Report 2020, https://worldhappiness.report/ed/2020/.

CHAPTER 13

Kristof, Nicholas, "The Four Secrets of Success," *The New York Times*, December 7, 2019.

ABOUT THE AUTHOR

TODD MILLER is an American-born entertainment executive who played a pioneering role in Asia's media development for over a quarter century. In senior leadership with a major Hollywood studio and as CEO of Asia's largest independent regional broadcaster, Miller has led multimillion dollar businesses in one of the world's most dynamic and diverse regions.

Miller has also experimented imaginatively with the work-life equation. While scaling the corporate ladder, he skillfully structured two sabbaticals, intentionally created a family through adoption, cycled coast-to-coast across two continents in support of children's charities, and explored more than one hundred countries on all seven continents.

Drawing on *ENRICH* principles, Miller built time wealth and passive income while working full time. He retired at age fifty-three and now lives on the Andaman Sea in Southern Thailand, in a beach house he custom built with his partner.

Miller devotes his time to enriching connections with people and projects.